Coping with Stress

ISSUES

Volume 206

Series Editor
Lisa Firth

Independence
Educational Publishers
Cambridge

First published by Independence
The Studio, High Green
Great Shelford
Cambridge CB22 5EG
England

British Library Cataloguing in Publication Data
Coping with stress. -- (Issues ; v. 206)
1. Stress (Psychology) 2. Stress in adolescence. 3. Stress
management for teenagers.
I. Series II. Firth, Lisa.
155.9'042-dc22

ISBN-13: 978 1 86168 582 7

Printed in Great Britain
MWL Print Group Ltd

CONTENTS

Chapter 1 Stress and Anxiety

Chapter 2 Causes of Stress

Chapter 3 Learning to Cope

OTHER TITLES IN THE ISSUES SERIES

For more on these titles, visit: **www.independence.co.uk**

Vegetarian and Vegan Diets ISBN 978 1 86168 406 6
Sustainability and Environment ISBN 978 1 86168 419 6
The Terrorism Problem ISBN 978 1 86168 420 2
Religious Beliefs ISBN 978 1 86168 421 9
A Classless Society? ISBN 978 1 86168 422 6
Migration and Population ISBN 978 1 86168 423 3
Climate Change ISBN 978 1 86168 424 0
Euthanasia and the Right to Die ISBN 978 1 86168 439 4
Sexual Orientation and Society ISBN 978 1 86168 440 0
The Gender Gap ISBN 978 1 86168 441 7
Domestic Abuse ISBN 978 1 86168 442 4
Travel and Tourism ISBN 978 1 86168 443 1
The Problem of Globalisation ISBN 978 1 86168 444 8
The Internet Revolution ISBN 978 1 86168 451 6
An Ageing Population ISBN 978 1 86168 452 3
Poverty and Exclusion ISBN 978 1 86168 453 0
Waste Issues ISBN 978 1 86168 454 7
Staying Fit ISBN 978 1 86168 455 4
Drugs in the UK ISBN 978 1 86168 456 1
The AIDS Crisis ISBN 978 1 86168 468 4
Bullying Issues ISBN 978 1 86168 469 1
Marriage and Cohabitation ISBN 978 1 86168 470 7
Our Human Rights ISBN 978 1 86168 471 4
Privacy and Surveillance ISBN 978 1 86168 472 1
The Animal Rights Debate ISBN 978 1 86168 473 8
Body Image and Self-Esteem ISBN 978 1 86168 484 4
Abortion – Rights and Ethics ISBN 978 1 86168 485 1
Racial and Ethnic Discrimination ISBN 978 1 86168 486 8
Sexual Health ISBN 978 1 86168 487 5
Selling Sex ISBN 978 1 86168 488 2
Citizenship and Participation ISBN 978 1 86168 489 9
Health Issues for Young People ISBN 978 1 86168 500 1
Crime in the UK ISBN 978 1 86168 501 8
Reproductive Ethics ISBN 978 1 86168 502 5
Tackling Child Abuse ISBN 978 1 86168 503 2
Money and Finances ISBN 978 1 86168 504 9
The Housing Issue ISBN 978 1 86168 505 6
Teenage Conceptions ISBN 978 1 86168 523 0
Work and Employment ISBN 978 1 86168 524 7
Understanding Eating Disorders ISBN 978 1 86168 525 4
Student Matters ISBN 978 1 86168 526 1
Cannabis Use ISBN 978 1 86168 527 8
Health and the State ISBN 978 1 86168 528 5
Tobacco and Health ISBN 978 1 86168 539 1
The Homeless Population ISBN 978 1 86168 540 7
Coping with Depression ISBN 978 1 86168 541 4
The Changing Family ISBN 978 1 86168 542 1
Bereavement and Grief ISBN 978 1 86168 543 8
Endangered Species ISBN 978 1 86168 544 5
Responsible Drinking ISBN 978 1 86168 555 1
Alternative Medicine ISBN 978 1 86168 560 5
Censorship Issues ISBN 978 1 86168 558 2
Living with Disability ISBN 978 1 86168 557 5
Sport and Society ISBN 978 1 86168 559 9
Self-Harming and Suicide ISBN 978 1 86168 556 8
Sustainable Transport ISBN 978 1 86168 572 8
Mental Wellbeing ISBN 978 1 86168 573 5
Child Exploitation ISBN 978 1 86168 574 2
The Gambling Problem ISBN 978 1 86168 575 9
The Energy Crisis ISBN 978 1 86168 576 6
Nutrition and Diet ISBN 978 1 86168 577 3
Coping with Stress ISBN 978 1 86168 582 7
Consumerism and Ethics ISBN 978 1 86168 583 4
Genetic Modification ISBN 978 1 86168 584 1
Education and Society ISBN 978 1 86168 585 8
The Media ISBN 978 1 86168 586 5
Biotechnology and Cloning ISBN 978 1 86168 587 2

A note on critical evaluation

Because the information reprinted here is from a number of different sources, readers should bear in mind the origin of the text and whether the source is likely to have a particular bias when presenting information (just as they would if undertaking their own research). It is hoped that, as you read about the many aspects of the issues explored in this book, you will critically evaluate the information presented. It is important that you decide whether you are being presented with facts or opinions. Does the writer give a biased or an unbiased report? If an opinion is being expressed, do you agree with the writer?

Coping with Stress offers a useful starting point for those who need convenient access to information about the many issues involved. However, it is only a starting point. Following each article is a URL to the relevant organisation's website, which you may wish to visit for further information.

Stress

Information from NHS Choices.

Introduction

Stress is the feeling of being under pressure. A little bit of pressure can:

- increase productivity;
- be motivating;
- improve performance.

However, too much pressure or prolonged pressure can lead to stress, which is unhealthy for the mind and body. It can cause symptoms such as:

- difficulty sleeping;
- sweating;
- lack of appetite;
- difficulty concentrating.

How common is stress?

It is difficult to estimate how common stress is because not everyone who has stress visits their GP. However, research suggests that a quarter of all adults will have a mental health problem, such as depression or anxiety, at some point in their lives. The same issues that contribute to these conditions, such as divorce and unemployment, may also cause stress.

A recent survey estimated that during 2008 and 2009, over 400,000 people in Britain experienced work-related stress that was making them unwell. Another survey from 2009 found that around one in six workers thought that their job was stressful.

Outlook

It may be possible to manage short-term stress using relaxation techniques, such as listening to music. Making changes at work or home may also help by removing the cause of stress. See the Live Well section about stress management on the NHS Choices website for further tips and advice.

If stress is not treated, it may cause further health problems such as:

- high blood pressure (hypertension);
- anxiety;
- depression.

These conditions may require further treatment, including medications such as antidepressants or talking therapies such as counselling.

Symptoms of stress

Stress affects different people in different ways and everyone has a different method of dealing with it.

The hormones (chemicals) that are released by your body as a result of stress can build up over time and cause various mental and physical symptoms. These are listed below.

Mental symptoms

Mental symptoms of stress (that affect your mind) include:

- anger
- depression
- anxiety
- changes in behaviour
- food cravings
- lack of appetite
- frequent crying
- difficulty sleeping (due to mental health problems)

NHS CHOICES

- feeling tired
- difficulty concentrating.

Physical symptoms

Physical symptoms of stress (that affect your body) include:

- chest pains
- constipation (an inability to empty your bowels)
- diarrhoea (passing loose, watery stools)
- cramps or muscle spasms, when your muscles contract (shorten) painfully
- dizziness
- fainting spells, where you temporarily lose consciousness
- biting your nails
- nervous twitches
- pins and needles (paraesthesia), a cold, burning, prickling or tingling sensation in your arms, legs, hands or feet
- feeling restless
- sweating more
- sexual difficulties, such as erectile dysfunction (an inability to get or maintain an erection) or a loss of sexual desire
- breathlessness
- muscular aches
- difficulty sleeping (due to physical problems).

Long-term symptoms

Experiencing even one or two of these symptoms can make you feel anxious or frustrated. This can be a vicious circle. For example, you want to avoid stress, but symptoms such as frequent crying or nervous twitching can make you feel annoyed with yourself and even more stressed.

If you have experienced some of these symptoms for a long time, you are at risk of developing high blood pressure (hypertension). This can lead to:

- a heart attack: a serious medical emergency where the supply of blood to your heart is suddenly blocked, usually by a blood clot.
- a stroke: a serious medical condition that occurs when the blood supply to the brain is interrupted.

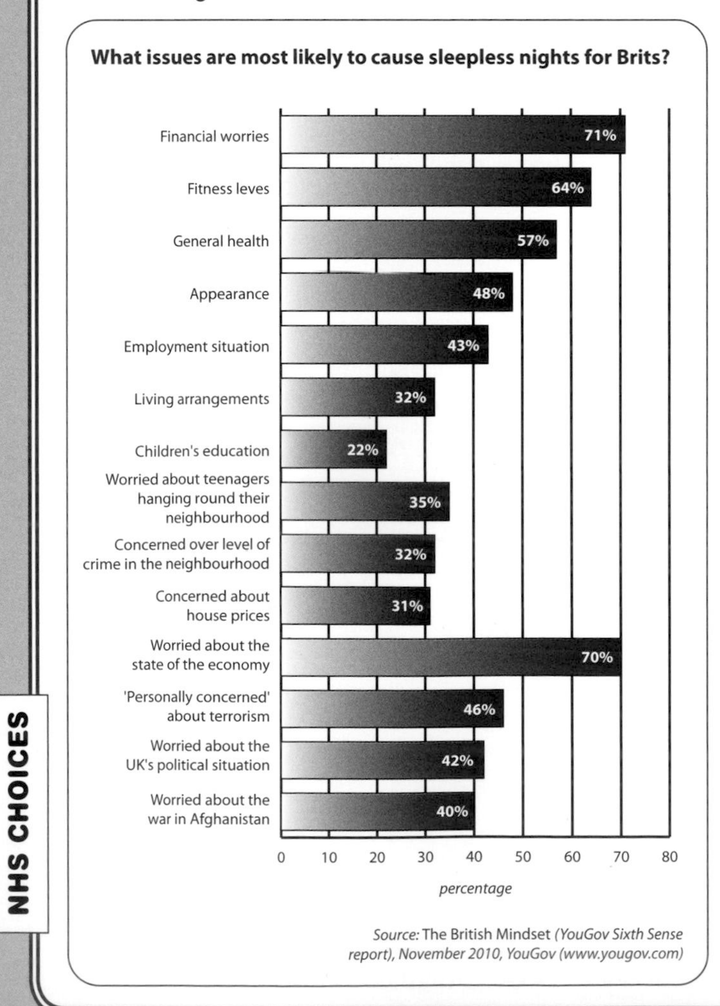

Source: The British Mindset *(YouGov Sixth Sense report), November 2010, YouGov (www.yougov.com)*

Treating stress

Some people are often unwilling to ask for help if they feel stressed. They may be embarrassed or think that they should be able to deal with stress on their own. However, if you are stressed, it is important to speak to someone about how you feel, particularly if it is interfering with your daily life.

Speak to your GP if you are stressed and under too much pressure. Speaking to someone about your feelings may help you identify what is causing your stress, which is a positive step.

Your GP may suggest that you try some self-help techniques, such as exercise, or they may recommend other treatments, such as a talking therapy.

Your treatment may depend on:

- the underlying cause of your stress;
- the symptoms you are experiencing;
- whether or not you have been diagnosed with any other conditions.

Counselling

Counselling involves talking to someone about a range of issues, such as what causes you to feel stressed. A counsellor will encourage you to discuss your feelings and they can help you find solutions to your problems. They can also help you discover ways to deal with stress and its effects.

NHS CHOICES

Cognitive behavioural therapy

Cognitive behavioural therapy (CBT) describes a number of therapies that are designed to solve problems. CBT starts with the idea that your problems are often created by you. It is not the situation itself that is making you unhappy, but how you think about it and react to it.

CBT aims to change the way that you think about a situation, as well as influencing your behaviour.

Anger management

Stress can cause you to feel angry. Anger management is a form of counselling that encourages you to deal with anger in a healthy way. It includes:

- recognising when you get angry;
- taking time to cool down;
- reducing your general stress levels in life.

Support groups

There are a number of independent support groups that help people recognise and overcome stress. Your GP may be able to give you details of support groups in your area.

For example, the mental health charity Mind has a network of local associations. No Panic, a charity for people who have panic attacks, phobias or anxiety, also has a network of local support groups, although there is a membership charge.

Medication

Medication may be used if your stress leads to further problems and you are diagnosed with:

- depression: when you have feelings of extreme sadness, despair or inadequacy that last for a long time.
- anxiety: constant feelings of unease, such as worry or fear, that affect your daily life.

Depression

If you have depression, you may be prescribed antidepressant medicines. The neurotransmitters (chemicals that carry messages between brain cells) do not work properly in people with depression.

Antidepressant medication boosts the activity of neurotransmitters so that brain signals function effectively and your mood is stabilised.

Anxiety

Several medications may be used to treat anxiety. They include:

- sedatives, which help you relax and calm you down;
- antihistamines, which have a calming effect on your brain;
- certain types of antidepressants.

Self-help

If you are feeling stressed, the tips below may be useful.

- Work out what situations make you feel stressed and how you behave in those situations. See if there is a way of managing those pressures so that you can face them in a different way.
- Make a list of all the things that make life stressful and a list of things that would help make life less stressful. This can help you sort out how you feel about certain situations.

NHS CHOICES

- If you feel that problems keep on building up and are making you more stressed, tell someone about it.

More information about beating stress can be found in the Live Well section about stress management on the NHS Choices website. This includes articles about:

- exercise to relieve stress;
- relaxation tips for stress;
- time management;
- credit crunch stress.

Complications of stress

If you experience stress over a long period, or you have severe stress, you may develop other conditions as a result. These conditions can include:

- depression: feelings of extreme sadness, despair or inadequacy that last for a long time.
- anxiety: constant feelings of unease, such as worry or fear, that affect your daily life.
- insomnia: difficulty getting to sleep or staying asleep
- high blood pressure (hypertension).
- stomach and duodenal ulcers (open sores that develop in the stomach or small intestine).
- asthma: a condition that causes inflammation (swelling) of the airways in the lungs.
- rheumatoid arthritis: a condition that causes pain and swelling in the joints, initially in the hands and feet but any joint may later become affected.
- an overactive thyroid gland (hyperthyroidism).

Cardiovascular disease

If it is not treated, high blood pressure can cause many different types of cardiovascular disease (conditions that affect your heart and circulation), including:

- stroke: a serious condition where the blood supply to the brain is interrupted.
- heart attack: a serious condition where the blood supply to the heart is blocked.
- blood clot (thrombosis): a serious condition that is caused by blood clots within the blood vessels.
- aneurysm: a serious condition that is caused by a weakness in the blood vessel wall, which forms a bulge in the blood vessel.

'The mental fog was awful'

Today, Liz Tucker is a health and wellbeing counsellor specialising in stress management. 14 years ago, at the age of 30, she burned out from work-related stress.

'I had a building company at the time and was working incredibly hard. It wasn't unusual for me to drive from Taunton, up to York and down to Norfolk in the space of 24 hours. I'd start work at 7am and often wouldn't finish until 8pm the following day, 36 hours later. In fact, the year I burned out, I drove over 100,000 miles.

'I loved the buzz of it. There was a lot of stress involved, but I really enjoyed the adrenaline kick of having something turn out right in the end. It was very satisfying.

'At first the work was manageable. Then, during the year before I became ill, I started working at weekends. I had no social life at all, which didn't bother me at the time.

'Then I met my partner and, because of the pressures of trying to see him and keep on top of the work, it all began to fall apart. I started feeling really tired and very lethargic. One Sunday night I went to bed early because I felt like I was getting a bit of a cold.

'When I woke on Monday, I simply couldn't get out of bed. I could move my fingers, head and feet, but I had no energy in my arms and legs.

'When the doctor told me I'd burned myself out from too much stress, I found it difficult to believe. To me, stress meant being unhappy, whereas I was really enjoying my life. But it was true: there was no work-life balance and I was living a high-stress life.

'In addition, my diet was appalling. I lived on food that I bought in petrol stations, and I hadn't been getting nearly enough sleep. My body had shut itself down in protest.

'For the next three months, I couldn't get out of bed. All I did was sleep. Very slowly, I began to improve but then, after a few months, the doctor diagnosed ME. I was housebound.

'The physical symptoms were bad but the mental "fog" was awful. It was like someone had drilled a hole in my head and filled it with concrete.

'I was like this for four years, and I was declining. My partner was beginning to wonder whether I was going to die, and when he asked the doctor, the answer was, "I simply don't know. She has the body of an 80-year-old". It was very shocking to hear.

'I think, up until that point, I'd believed the doctors knew what was right for me. So hearing that they didn't know what to do made me start thinking about my own future. With my partner, I began thinking about what was right for me to do.

'I decided I needed some pleasure in life. I had been so worried for so long. I began having a weekly massage and hypnotherapy to help me relax. I also decided not to watch anything on TV that was violent or miserable.

'The biggest turning point was when I began to pace myself. Up until then, I'd compare myself to how I was before. If I was feeling a bit better, I would try to do lots of things and then feel ill with exhaustion again. I began to realise I was setting myself unrealistic goals so I decided to take things gradually.

'After I'd started this regime of proper relaxing, it was remarkable how quickly I began to feel better. I was eating a healthy diet with lots of fruit and vegetables and I'd stopped having caffeine and alcohol. I began to notice the changes within a few weeks.

'After three months, I was feeling so much better, but because I'd spent so much time in bed, I was very weak physically.

'After six months, I was back to normal. I had lots of energy, my skin was better and I didn't have to stay in bed the whole time. It was amazing.

'I've now been working as a health and wellbeing counsellor for ten years. I went back to university and studied human health and biology, really just to find out what had happened to me. I found it so interesting it has turned into my career.

'I'm working really hard again and get a lot of satisfaction out of it, but the difference is that now I have a work-life balance and know what to do when things get too stressful.'

➪ The above information is reprinted with kind permission from the Department of Health. Visit www.nhs.uk for more information.

Facts about stress

Information from the International Stress Management Association UK.

Most official statistics on stress are two years old at best and statistics from other sources vary widely.

Here are just a few:

- ➪ Stress and chronic ill health in the workplace costs £100 billion [per year] – *Dame Carole Black, ISMA Conference 2009*
- ➪ An estimated 442,000 individuals in Britain who worked in 2007/08 believed that they were experiencing work-related stress at a level that was making them ill – *Labour Force Survey Government Stats*
- ➪ Estimates indicate that self-reported work-related stress, depression or anxiety accounted for an estimated 13.5 million lost working days in Britain in 2007/08 – *Labour Force Survey*
- ➪ Direct cost of sickness absence estimated as £635 per person per year – *CIPD 2008*
- ➪ Indirect costs of sickness absence have been measured as twice the direct costs, i.e. £1,270, making a total of £1,905 per employee per year: typically around 9% of payroll costs – *Norwich Union Healthcare*
- ➪ In 2008, for every 80p spent on health promotion and intervention programmes, £4 can be saved due to reduced absenteeism, temporary staff, presenteeism and improved motivation – *The European Network for Workplace Health Promotion*
- ➪ The 2007 Psychosocial Working Conditions (PWC) survey indicated that around 13.6% of all working individuals thought their job was very or extremely stressful – *Health and Safety Executive*
- ➪ The annual incidence of work-related mental health problems in Britain in 2007 was approximately 5,750 new cases per year. However, this almost certainly underestimates the true incidence of these conditions in the British workforce – *Health and Safety Executive*
- ➪ According to self-reports, an estimated 237,000 people who worked in 2008 first became aware of work-related stress, depression or anxiety giving an annual incidence rate of 780 cases per 100,000 workers – *Labour Force Survey*
- ➪ Employee absence levels in public sector at 9.6 days per annum per employee whilst private sector absence at 6.6 days per annum per employee – *CIPD Absence Management survey 2010*
- ➪ Despite pressure to cut costs, 22% of organisations have increased their spend on employee well-being, with only 9% showing a reduction. Those who have increased spending in 2010 have indicated they are likely to increase their wellbeing spend further in 2011 – *CIPD Absence Management Survey 2010*

➪ The above information is reprinted with kind permission from the International Stress Management Association UK. Visit www.isma.org.uk for more information.

The stigma of stress

Although it is slowly dying out, there is still, for many, a stigma about stress. People are, on the whole, not keen to admit to it.

- Three out of four men in Britain say they would not go to the GP if they were under stress as they would be afraid that the GP would think that they are 'unbalanced' or 'neurotic'.
- There is a strong link to social factors, with stigma being stronger amongst working-class men. This may be a reason for men being three times more likely to have a drink problem than women. They may have been afraid to go to the doctor with a stress problem and tried to cope with it by drinking.
- A Scottish Public Attitudes Survey on Mental Health in 2002 found that half of all those who took part said that they would not want anyone to know if they developed a mental health problem.
- About the same number of people thought that the media portrayal of people with mental health problems was more negative than positive.
- Often, people don't think it is stress. Many go to the GP to get help for a body symptom – headaches, upset stomach, heart racing, etc. Some feel quite angry if they are told it is stress.
- If you do feel like this, you may feel stress is a shameful thing. This sense of shame then feeds the stress. The stress makes the sense of shame worse, and so on. This acts like a vicious circle – one thing feeds the other.
- You may have learned to put on a mask to hide stress. This often lets stress build up as often just talking about it can help. It also stops you from seeing how common it is. People often say that once they open up to friends, the friends tell them they also have stress.

Most people would rather have a broken leg than stress. It is easy to see why this is. Compare the two using the table below.

Too many of us still think of a broken leg as a 'real' problem while stress is all in the mind. This suggests that all you need is a good shake and that, if you really wanted to, you could get rid of it. There are three points to be made here:

- No-one wants to have stress.
- The causes of stress are complex.
- The reasons that keep it going are complex.

If all you needed were to give yourself a good shake, you would gladly have done so. Don't let anyone get on at you for having stress – ask them to look at the Glasgow STEPS website instead. If they still get on at you then why worry about people who have such a simple view of life.

While views about mental health are changing and becoming more realistic, there is still a long way to go.

- The above information is reprinted with kind permission from Glasgow STEPS. Visit http://glasgowsteps.com for more information.

Broken leg vs stress

Broken leg	Stress
You will know what caused you to break your leg	You often do not know what caused stress
You (and others) can see what is wrong	Stress is often invisible – you may look fine on the outside
You will know what to do to make it better	You may not know what to do to make it better
You will know that it will mend	You may not know if it will get better (without help, stress often gets worse)
You will know how long it will take to mend	You may not see a future without stress
You will not feel guilty about having a broken leg	You may feel guilty about having stress (due to the stigma)

Source: Glasgow STEPS © Crown copyright – nhs.uk

NHS CHOICES

Work-related stress – signs and symptoms

Information from the Health and Safety Executive.

Key message

Stress can cause changes in those experiencing it. In some cases there are clear signs that people are experiencing stress at work and if these can be identified early, action can be taken before the pressure becomes a problem. This may make it easier to reduce and eliminate the causes.

It is important that everyone looks out for changes in a person's or a group's behaviour. However, in many cases the changes may only be noticeable to the person subject to the stress and so it is also important to look at how you are feeling and try to identify any potential issues you may have as early as possible and take positive action to address them; this may be raising the matter with a line manager, talking to an occupational health professional or your own GP.

Stress can show itself in many different ways – see below. Some of the items in this list may not be signs of stress if people always behave this way. Managers may need to manage staff exhibiting some of these signs differently. You are particularly looking for changes in the way people behave that could be linked with excessive pressures.

Male

Head and mental health

Short term: Anxious, changed moods, negative thoughts, more emotional, disturbed sleep patterns

Long term: Anxiety, depression

Heart, lungs and circulation

Short term: Changes in heart rate, increased blood pressure 'palpitations'

Long term: Hypertension (high blood pressure), heart disease

Skin

Short term: Sweating, reddening, blushing

Long term: Eczema, psoriasis

Metabolism

Short term: Mobilisation of energy sources, increased cholesterol in blood, increased glucose availability

Long term: Inefficient energy use, increased fat deposition, insulin resistance, metabolic syndrome

Muscles and joints

Short term: Increased blood flow to muscles, muscle tension

Long term: Loss of muscle function and structure, stiffness, soreness, regional pain syndromes, osteoporosis

In some cases there are clear signs that people are experiencing stress at work and if these can be identified early, action can be taken before the pressure becomes a problem

Digestive system and gut

Short term: 'Butterflies' in stomach, dry mouth, suppression of digestion/nausea

Long term: Appetite suppression, impaired capacity to repair ulcers, chronic dysfunction of the gut such as Irritable Bowel Syndrome

HEALTH AND SAFETY EXECUTIVE

Reproduction and growth

Short term: Suppression of reproductive and growth systems (hormones)

Long term: Reproductive abnormalities, decreased testosterone and erectile dysfunction, loss of libido

Immune system

Short term: Enhancement of specific immune responses – e.g. to deal with wounding

Long term: Eventual immune suppression – increased susceptibility to some infectious diseases

Female

Head and mental health

Short term: Anxious, changed moods, negative thoughts, more emotional, disturbed sleep patterns

Long term: Anxiety, depression

Heart, lungs and circulation

Short term: Changes in heart rate, increased blood pressure 'palpitations'

Long term: Hypertension (high blood pressure), heart disease

Skin

Short term: Sweating, reddening, blushing

Long term: Eczema, psoriasis

Metabolism

Short term: Mobilisation of energy sources, increased cholesterol in blood, increased glucose availability

Long term: Inefficient energy use, increased fat deposition, insulin resistance, metabolic syndrome

Muscles and joints

Short term: Increased blood flow to muscles, muscle tension

Long term: Loss of muscle function and structure, stiffness, soreness, regional pain syndromes, osteoporosis

Digestive system and gut

Short term: 'Butterflies' in stomach, dry mouth, suppression of digestion/nausea

Long term: Appetite suppression, impaired capacity to repair ulcers, chronic dysfunction of the gut such as Irritable Bowel Syndrome

Reproduction and growth

Short term: Suppression of reproductive and growth systems (hormones)

Long term: Irregular or loss of menstrual cycle, reproductive abnormalities, loss of libido

Immune system

Short term: Enhancement of specific immune responses – e.g. to deal with wounding

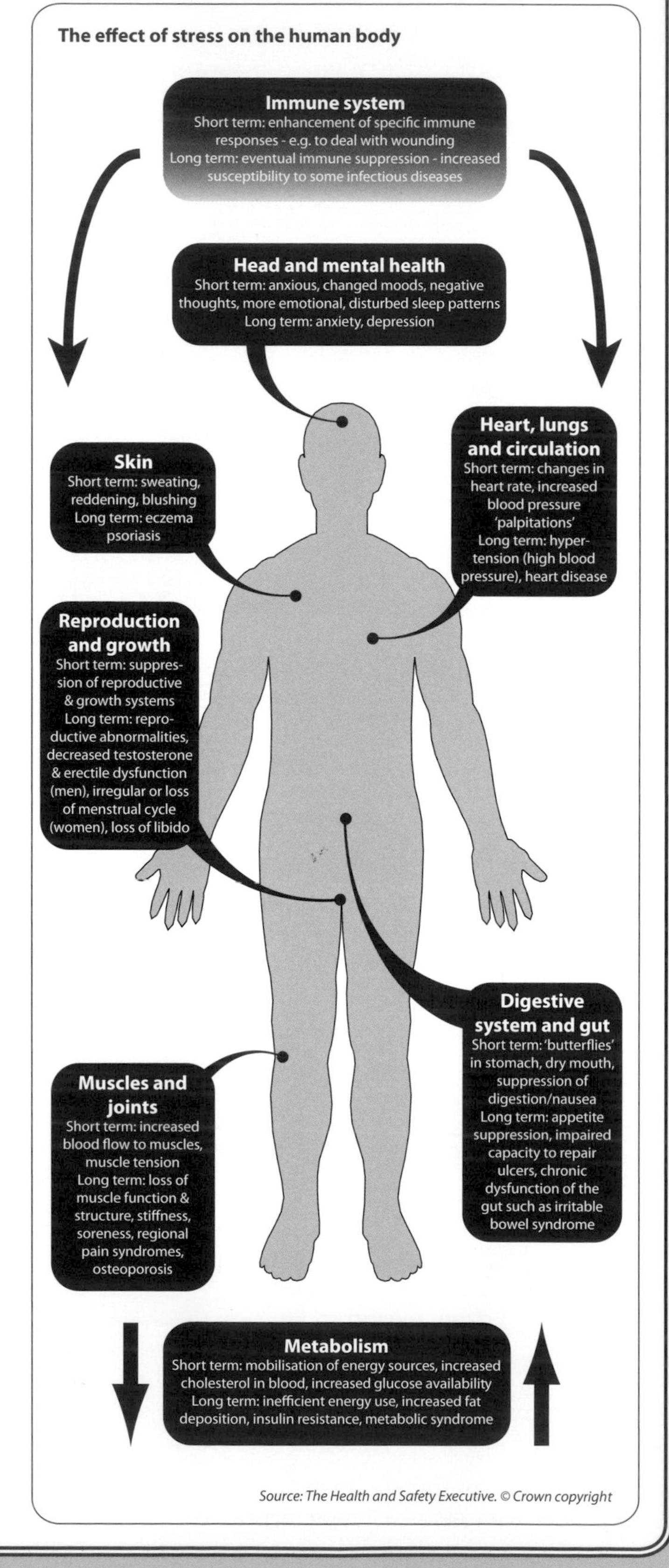

The effect of stress on the human body
Immune system
Short term: enhancement of specific immune responses - e.g. to deal with wounding
Long term: eventual immune suppression - increased susceptibility to some infectious diseases
Head and mental health
Short term: anxious, changed moods, negative thoughts, more emotional, disturbed sleep patterns
Long term: anxiety, depression
Skin
Short term: sweating, reddening, blushing
Long term: eczema psoriasis
Heart, lungs and circulation
Short term: changes in heart rate, increased blood pressure 'palpitations'
Long term: hyper-tension (high blood pressure), heart disease
Reproduction and growth
Short term: suppres-sion of reproductive & growth systems
Long term: repro-ductive abnormalities, decreased testosterone & erectile dysfunction (men), irregular or loss of menstrual cycle (women), loss of libido
Digestive system and gut
Short term: 'butterflies' in stomach, dry mouth, suppression of digestion/nausea
Long term: appetite suppression, impaired capacity to repair ulcers, chronic dysfunction of the gut such as irritable bowel syndrome
Muscles and joints
Short term: increased blood flow to muscles, muscle tension
Long term: loss of muscle function & structure, stiffness, soreness, regional pain syndromes, osteoporosis
Metabolism
Short term: mobilisation of energy sources, increased cholesterol in blood, increased glucose availability
Long term: inefficient energy use, increased fat deposition, insulin resistance, metabolic syndrome

Source: The Health and Safety Executive. © Crown copyright

HEALTH AND SAFETY EXECUTIVE

Long term: Eventual immune suppression – increased susceptibility to some infectious diseases

Signs of stress in individuals

If you are suffering from some of the following symptoms it may indicate that you are feeling the effects of stress. If you find that work or aspects of your work bring on or make these symptoms worse, speak to your line manager, trade union representative or your HR department. It may be that some action taken at an early stage will ease the stress and reduce or stop the symptoms.

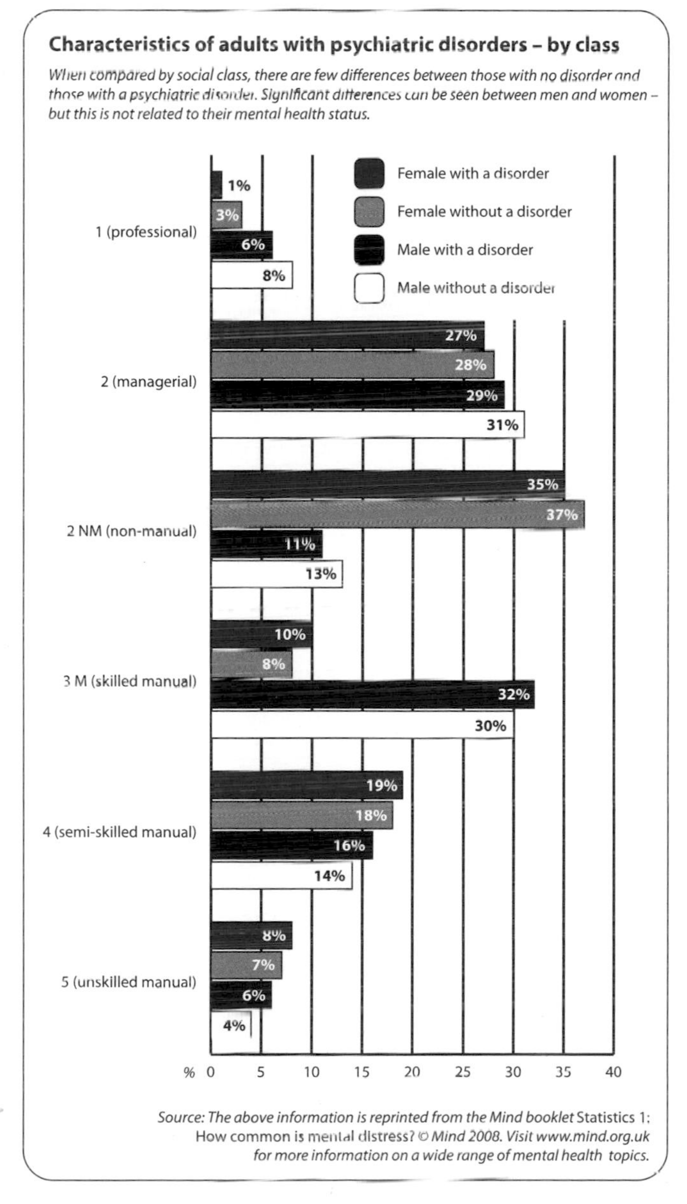

Emotional symptoms

- Negative or depressive feeling
- Disappointment with yourself
- Increased emotional reactions – more tearful or sensitive or aggressive
- Loneliness, withdrawn
- Loss of motivation, commitment and confidence
- Mood swings (not behavioural)

Mental symptoms

- Confusion, indecision
- Can't concentrate
- Poor memory

Changes from your normal behaviour

- Changes in eating habits
- Increased smoking, drinking or drug taking 'to cope'
- Mood swings affecting your behaviour
- Changes in sleep patterns
- Twitchy, nervous behaviour
- Changes in attendance, such as arriving later or taking more time off

Please note these are indicators of behaviour of those experiencing stress. They may also be indicative of other conditions. If you are concerned about yourself please seek advice from your GP. If you are concerned about a colleague try to convince them to see their GP.

Signs of stress in a group

- Disputes and disaffection within the group
- Increase in staff turnover
- Increase in complaints and grievances
- Increased sickness absence
- Increased reports of stress
- Difficulty in attracting new staff
- Poor performance
- Customer dissatisfaction or complaints

It is not up to you or your managers to diagnose stress. If you or they are very worried about a person, recommend they see their GP. It is up to you and your managers to recognise that behaviours have changed, be aware that something is wrong and take prompt action. Take care not to over-react to small changes in behaviour. You and your managers need to act when these behavioural changes continue. Use these symptoms (both individual and group) as clues.

- The above information is reprinted with kind permission from the Health and Safety Executive. Visit www.hse.gov.uk for more information.

Anxiety, panic and phobias

Information from the Royal College of Psychiatrists.

Introduction

Anxiety is something we all feel it when we are in a situation that is threatening or difficult. The anxiety goes away when we have got used to the situation, when the situation changes, or when we leave the situation.

If it just goes on and on, or if it happens out of the blue, or for no obvious reason, it can make life very difficult.

This article deals with anxiety in general, and with three particular kinds of anxiety:

- generalised anxiety disorder;
- panic attacks;
- phobias.

It is for anyone for whom anxiety is a problem – but also for friends and relatives who may want to understand more about it.

What is anxiety?

Anxiety feels like fear. When it's caused by a problem in our life that we can't solve, such as money difficulties, we call it worry. If it is a sudden reaction to an immediate threat, like looking over a cliff or being confronted by an angry dog, we call it fear.

Although these feelings are unpleasant, they exist for a purpose. Worry, fear and anxiety can all be helpful.

- Psychologically – they keep us alert and give us the motivation to plan and to deal with problems.
- Physically – they prepare our body for sudden, strenuous exercise, to run away from danger or to attack it – the 'fight or flight' response.

These feelings become a problem when they are too strong, or when they carry on even when we don't need them any more. They can make you uncomfortable, stop you from doing the things you want to – and can generally make life difficult.

How common are anxiety problems?

About one in every ten people will have troublesome anxiety or a phobia at some point in their lives. However, most of us never ask for treatment.

Are these feelings the same as 'stress'?

People talk about 'stress' when they feel they cannot cope with the pressures they are under in their lives. This can lead to problems like anxiety, depression and overuse of alcohol or drugs.

Isn't anxiety bad for you?

Actually, some anxiety is good for you. It keeps you alert and can help you to perform well. But only some. If it gets too intense, or goes on too long, it starts to interfere with your performance, can make you depressed and can damage your physical health.

Anxiety and physical health

Anxiety seems to be linked – although we don't understand how – with a number of medical conditions. In most cases, the anxiety seems to have come first. For example, older people with panic attacks seem to be more likely to have heart problems.

Symptoms of anxiety

In the mind:

- feeling worried all the time
- feeling tired
- unable to concentrate
- feeling irritable
- sleeping badly
- feeling depressed

In the body:

- fast or irregular heartbeats (palpitations)
- sweating
- face goes pale
- dry mouth
- muscle tension and pains
- trembling
- numbness or tingling
- breathing fast
- dizziness
- faintness
- indigestion
- passing water frequently

ROYAL COLLEGE OF PSYCHIATRISTS

- nausea, stomach cramps
- diarrhoea

It's easy to mistake these feelings for the symptoms of a serious physical illness – and if this makes you worry, the symptoms get even worse. Anxiety and panic are often accompanied by feelings of depression, when you start to feel down, lose your appetite and see the future as bleak and hopeless.

Generalised anxiety disorder (GAD)

You feel anxious all the time, not just in certain situations. If you have this high level of 'background' anxiety, you may also have panic attacks and some phobias (see below).

Panic attack

You get unpredictable and intense attacks of anxiety – often in a situation that you know is likely to make you anxious. Your symptoms of anxiety come on suddenly and reach a peak in ten minutes or less. You may also experience:

- fear of dying;
- fear of 'going crazy' or losing control;
- feeling short of breath;
- a choking sensation.

These attacks can be so sudden and violent that you think you are going to die. In fact, about a quarter of the people who go to an A&E department with chest pain will have had a panic attack.

Although the symptoms are much the same as those of GAD (see above), they are much more intense, come and go, and need different treatments.

Phobia

A fear of a situation or thing that is not actually dangerous and which most people do not find troublesome. The nearer you get to the situation or thing that makes you anxious, the more anxious you get ... and so you tend to avoid it. Away from the thing or situation that makes you feel anxious, you feel fine.

Common phobias include:

- agoraphobia – a fear of public places where escape seems difficult (like crowds, queues, buses, trains or bridges). It can stop you from leaving the house.
- social phobia – a fear of being with other people. You worry that people are judging you and that you will embarrass yourself. This can make it hard to eat out or speak to other people, particularly if you are meeting someone for the first time or at parties.
- specific phobias – such as a fear of spiders, needles, heights or flying.

The problem is that avoiding the situations that make you anxious will actually make the phobia worse as time goes on. Your life can become more and more dominated by the precautions you have to take to avoid the things that scare you. You will usually know that there is no real danger, you may feel silly about your fear, but still find that you can't control it. A phobia can start after a distressing or traumatic event – an attack by a dog can produce a dog phobia, for example.

What causes anxiety problems?

Genes

Some of us seem to be born with a tendency to be anxious – research suggests that it can be inherited through our genes. However, even people who are not naturally anxious can become anxious if they are put under enough pressure.

Misunderstanding symptoms

Some people start to believe that the physical symptoms of mild anxiety are the symptoms of a dangerous physical disease. This makes them worry more, so the symptoms get worse, so they worry more ... and so on.

Trauma

Sometimes it is obvious what is causing anxiety. When the problem disappears, so does the anxiety. However, there are some circumstances that are so upsetting and threatening that the anxiety they cause can go on long after the event.

These are often life-threatening situations like car crashes, train crashes or fires. The people involved can feel nervous and anxious for months or years after the event, even if they have been physically unharmed.

It can also happen after childhood neglect or abuse and persistent mistreatment or torture in adult life. This is part of what we now call post-traumatic stress disorder.

Drugs

Sometimes anxiety may be caused by using street drugs like amphetamines, LSD or ecstasy. Even the caffeine in coffee can be enough to make some of us feel uncomfortably anxious!

Mental health problems

Many mental health problems can make you anxious. About half of people with depression get panic attacks at some point.

Physical problems

Some physical problems, like thyroid disease, can make you feel anxious.

Some or all of the above...

It may not be clear at all why you feel anxious, because

ROYAL COLLEGE OF PSYCHIATRISTS

it is due to a mixture of your personality, the things that have happened to you, or big changes in your life.

Helping yourself

- Be practical – anxiety is a normal part of being human – and is often there for a good reason. We cannot remove all worry from our lives. If you are facing a practical problem in your life, it's best to get some practical help with it. For example, Relate offers counselling for relationship difficulties and Citizens Advice Bureaux help with sorting out money problems.
- Talk about the problem – this can help when the anxiety comes from recent knocks like a partner leaving, a child becoming ill or losing a job. Who should you talk to? Try friends or relatives whom you trust and respect, and who are good listeners. They may have had the same problem themselves, or know someone else who has. As well as having the chance to talk, you may be able to find out how other people have coped with the problem.

About one in every ten people will have troublesome anxiety or a phobia at some point in their lives. However, most of us never ask for treatment

- Self-help groups – these are a good way of getting in touch with people with similar problems. They can understand what you are going through and may be able to suggest ways of coping. These groups may be focussed on anxieties and phobias, or may be made up of people who have been through similar experiences – women's groups, bereaved parents' groups, survivors of abuse groups.
- Learning to relax – it sounds too obvious: surely everyone can relax? But if your anxiety just won't go away, it can be really helpful to learn some special ways of relaxing, to help you to be a bit more in control of your anxiety and tension. You can learn these through groups, with professionals, but there are also books and DVDs you can use to teach yourself these techniques. It's a good idea to practise this regularly, not just at times of crisis.
- Do some exercise – several studies have found that regular exercise seems to lower levels of anxiety.
- Bibliotherapy – using a self-help book. There is good evidence that this works well for many people. Most of the books now on the market use the principles of Cognitive behavioural therapy (CBT).

Family and friends

Someone with anxiety and phobias may not talk about their feelings, even with family or close friends. Even so, it is usually obvious that things are not right. The sufferer will tend to look pale and tense, and may be easily startled by normal sounds such as a door-bell ringing or a car's horn.

They will also tend to be irritable and this can cause arguments with those close to them, especially if they do not understand why the sufferer feels that they cannot do certain things. Although friends and family can understand the distress caused by anxiety, they can find it difficult to live with, especially if the fears seem unreasonable.

Getting help

If you have an anxiety problem which just won't go away, it's worth getting help. You may not want to ask for help because you worry that people might think you are 'mad'. In fact, people with anxiety and fears don't often have a serious mental illness. It's much better to get help as soon as you can rather than suffer in silence.

Cognitive behavioural therapy

This is a talking treatment which can help us to understand how 'habits of thinking' can be making anxiety worse – or even causing it:

- jumping to the conclusion that something bad is going to happen.
- automatically thinking that the worst possible thing is going to happen.

These are both very powerful ways of making yourself feel anxious – and yet they aren't realistic. Yes, bad things do sometimes happen and the worst does sometimes happen – but not always or even usually.

CBT can help you to change these 'extreme' ways of thinking, which can also help you to feel better and to behave differently.

Another helpful idea is mindfulness – a way of seeing unhelpful worries as 'just' thoughts. This means that, instead of being tormented by worries, you can learn to accept them and 'let go'.

Helping phobias

Graded exposure involves facing our fears one step at a time. It works because, if you spend time in any feared situation, your anxiety will eventually decrease and go away.

For example, Kate had a fear of birds. She wrote a list of situations that she needed to face, from the easiest to the most difficult to tackle – her anxiety 'ladder':

ROYAL COLLEGE OF PSYCHIATRISTS

1 put picture of robin on bedroom wall
2 watch TV documentary on birds
3 visit pet shop and stand next to caged parrot
4 walk in local park past duck pond
5 walk in park, sit on bench and feed ducks.

She practised spending enough time with each step on her 'anxiety ladder' again and again until her anxiety ebbed away. Once she could tackle a step without feeling anxious, she moved on to the next step.

This treatment can take place in groups or individually, and is usually weekly for several weeks or months. Psychotherapists may or may not be medically qualified.

Computerised CBT

There are now a number of computer programs which you can use to give yourself CBT. NICE recommend a program called 'FearFighter' for panic or phobia. You can get this through your GP.

If this is not enough, there are several different kinds of professionals who may be able to help – the GP, psychiatrist, psychologist, social worker, nurse or counsellor.

Medication

Medication can play a part in the treatment of some people with anxiety or phobias.

The most common tranquillisers are the valium-like drugs, the benzodiazepines (most sleeping tablets also belong to this class of drugs). They are very effective at relieving anxiety, but we now know that they can be addictive after only four weeks of regular use. When people try to stop taking them, they may experience unpleasant withdrawal symptoms which can go on for some time. These drugs should be only used for short periods of up to two weeks in generalised anxiety, perhaps to help during a crisis. They should not be used for longer-term treatment of anxiety and should not be used at all in panic disorder.

Antidepressants can help to relieve anxiety as well as the depression for which they are usually prescribed. They usually take two to four weeks to work and have to be taken regularly to work properly. One of the newer SSRI antidepressants would usually be tried first – if that is not helpful, one of the older tricyclic antidepressants can be tried, or a newer antidepressant called Venlafaxine.

Beta-blockers are drugs usually used to treat high blood pressure. In low doses, they can sometimes control the physical shaking of anxiety. They can be taken shortly before meeting people or before speaking in public, or having to perform.

Herbal remedies

Studies suggest that *Valeriana officinalis* (valerian) does not seem to be helpful in anxiety, although *Matricaria recutita* (German chamomile) and *Melissa officinalis* (lemon balm) 'show promise'. *Piper methysticum* (kava) does seem to be effective, but is currently banned in the UK because of worries that it may be toxic to the liver.

Which treatments work best?

The treatments that seem to work for the longest time are, in descending order:

- psychological therapy (CBT);
- pharmacological therapy (an SSRI);
- self-help (bibliotherapy based on CBT principles).

Anxiety and phobias in children

Most children go through times when they feel very frightened about things. It's a normal part of growing up. For instance, toddlers get very attached to the people who look after them. If for any reason they are separated from them, they can become very anxious or upset.

Many children are scared of the dark or of imaginary monsters. These fears usually disappear as a child grows older, and they do not usually spoil the child's life or interfere with their development. Most will feel anxious about important events like their first day at school, but they stop being frightened afterwards and are able to get on and enjoy their new situation.

Teenagers often feel anxious. They tend to be worried about how they look, what other people think of them, how they get on with people in general, but especially about how they get on with the opposite sex. These worries can usually be helped by talking about them. However, if they are too strong, other people may notice that they are doing badly at school, behaving differently, or feeling physically unwell.

If a child or teenager feels so anxious or fearful that it is spoiling their life, it's a good thing to ask your GP to look into it.

This leaflet was produced by the Royal College of Psychiatrists' Public Education Editorial Board.
Series editor: Dr Philip Timms
Expert review: Dr Paul Blenkiron

⇨ The above information is reprinted with kind permission from the Royal College of Psychiatrists. Visit www.rcpsych.ac.uk for more information on this and other related topics.

Generalised anxiety disorder (GAD)

Generalised anxiety disorder is a condition where you have excessive anxiety on most days. The most effective treatment is thought to be cognitive behavioural therapy (CBT). Other treatment options include antidepressant medicines, and sometimes other types of medicines.

What is anxiety?

When you are anxious you feel fearful and tense. In addition you may also have one or more unpleasant physical symptoms. For example: a fast heart rate, palpitations, feeling sick, shaking (tremor), sweating, dry mouth, chest pain, headaches, fast breathing. The physical symptoms are partly caused by the brain, which sends lots of messages down nerves to various parts of the body when we are anxious. The nerve messages tend to make the heart, lungs, and other parts of the body work faster. In addition, you release stress hormones (such as adrenaline) into the bloodstream when you are anxious. These can also act on the heart, muscles and other parts of the body to cause symptoms.

Anxiety is normal in stressful situations, and can even be helpful. For example, most people will be anxious when threatened by an aggressive person. The burst of adrenaline and nerve impulses which we have in response to stressful situations can encourage a 'fight or flight' response. Some people are more prone to normal anxieties. For example, some people are more anxious before examinations than others. Anxiety is abnormal if it:

- is out of proportion to the stressful situation, or
- persists when a stressful situation has gone, or the stress is minor, or
- appears for no apparent reason when there is no stressful situation.

What are anxiety disorders?

There are various conditions (disorders) where anxiety is a main symptom. This article is about generalised anxiety disorder (GAD). There is information on our website – www.patient.co.uk – about other types of anxiety disorders (such as panic disorder, phobias, acute reaction to stress, post-traumatic stress disorder, etc.).

What is generalised anxiety disorder?

If you have generalised anxiety disorder (GAD) you have a lot of anxiety (feeling fearful, worried and tense) on most days. The condition persists long-term. Some of the physical symptoms of anxiety (detailed above) may come and go. Your anxiety tends to be about various stresses at home or work, often about quite minor things. Sometimes you do not know why you are anxious.

It can be difficult to tell the difference between normal mild anxiety in someone with an anxious personality, and someone with GAD. As a rule, symptoms of GAD cause you distress and affect your day-to-day activities. In addition, you will usually have some of the following symptoms:

- Feeling restless, on edge, irritable, muscle tension, or keyed up a lot of the time.
- Tiring easily.
- Difficulty concentrating and your mind going blank quite often.
- Poor sleep (insomnia). Usually it is difficulty in getting off to sleep.

You do not have GAD if your anxiety is about one specific thing. For example, if your anxiety is usually caused by fear of one thing then you are more likely to have a phobia.

Who gets generalised anxiety disorder?

GAD develops in about one in 50 people at some stage in life. Twice as many women as men are affected. It usually first develops in your 20s and is less common in older people.

What causes generalised anxiety disorder?

The cause is not clear. The condition often develops for no apparent reason. Various factors may play a part. For example:

- Your genetic makeup may be important. Some people have a tendency to have an anxious personality, which can run in families.
- Childhood traumas such as abuse, or death of a parent, may make you more prone to anxiety when you become older.
- A major stress in life may trigger the condition. For example, a family crisis or a major civilian trauma

PATIENT UK

such as a toxic chemical spill. But the symptoms then persist when any trigger has gone. Common minor stresses in life, which you may otherwise have easily coped with, may then keep the symptoms going once the condition has been triggered.

Some people who have other mental health problems such as depression or schizophrenia may also develop GAD.

How is generalised anxiety disorder diagnosed?

If the typical symptoms develop and persist for at least six months, then a doctor can usually be confident that you have GAD. However, it is sometimes difficult to tell if you have GAD, panic disorder, depression, or a mixture of these conditions.

GAD develops in about one in 50 people at some stage in life. Twice as many women as men are affected. It usually first develops in your 20s and is less common in older people

Some of the physical symptoms of anxiety can be caused by physical problems which can be confused with anxiety. So, sometimes other conditions may need to be ruled out. For example:

- Drinking a lot of caffeine (in tea, coffee and cola).
- The side-effect of some prescribed medicines. For example, selective serotonin reuptake inhibitor (SSRI) antidepressants.
- An overactive thyroid gland.
- Taking some street drugs.
- Certain heart conditions which cause palpitations (uncommon).
- Low blood sugar level (rare).
- Tumours which make too much adrenaline and other similar hormones (very rare).

What is the outlook (prognosis)?

Without treatment, GAD tends to persist throughout life. It is relatively mild in some cases, but for some it can be very disabling. The results from one clinic showed that at the end of 12 years four out of ten people had recovered. The outlook was worse for people who had more than one anxiety disorder.

The severity of symptoms tends to wax and wane with some good spells, and some not so good spells. Symptoms may flare up and become worse for a while during periods of major life stresses. For example, if you lose your job, or split up with your partner.

People with GAD are more likely than average to smoke heavily, drink too much alcohol and take street drugs. Each of these things may ease anxiety symptoms in the short-term. However, addiction to nicotine, alcohol or drugs makes things worse in the long-term, and can greatly affect your general health and wellbeing.

Treatment can help to ease symptoms, and can improve your quality of life. However, there is no quick fix or complete cure.

- The above information is an extract from the Patient UK factsheet *Generalised Anxiety Disorder* and is reprinted with permission. Visit www.patient.co.uk for more information.

Employers are required by law to manage the workplace environment to reduce stress levels and look after the wellbeing of their employees. If you are feeling very stressed at or by work, talk to your manager. Your employer may be able to provide opportunities for you to develop some skills to help you cope with stress – such as relaxation, assertiveness or time-management skills.

You may also be able to get support through informal channels – for example, talking to a sympathetic colleague or a friend about workplace stress.

Money problems

Money problems can cause high levels of stress and depression. They can cause relationships to break up, people to lose their homes, and families to split up – all of which are additional sources of stress.

It is important to get advice on controlling debt early on, before problems become overwhelming. For help and advice, contact the Government's National Debtline on 0808 808 4000. A Citizens' Advice Bureau can advise you about the options available for dealing with any financial or housing problems (look them up in your local phone book).

Relationships

Relationships – with your partner, children, parents, friends, neighbours or work colleagues – don't always run smoothly, and can be the cause of considerable stress. If you don't have someone you can confide in and trust, this can add to any stress you are experiencing. And if you are having problems in one area of your life, it can put a strain on your relationships with everyone else.

Whatever the problem with a relationship, the first step towards dealing with it is to acknowledge it and try to work things through together. Try to talk through the issues, stay positive, look at what you can do to improve things, and accept that some things are outside your control. Reflect on your choices.

Major life events

Any major life change can be stressful. Stress may be triggered by unexpected events like losing a job, bereavement or illness, divorce or separation, or by planned changes such as getting married, moving house or having a baby (which is not always planned).

How you deal with the event will depend on how prepared you were for it, how long it lasts, and how much support you have. Sometimes several life events happen at once and this can 'tip your balance' from being moderately stressed to being unable to cope. Where possible, avoid taking on too many potentially stressful situations at once.

Time pressure

Be realistic about what you can achieve, learn to say 'No', and prioritise. Making time for leisure, exercise and holidays is just as essential as spending time on the things we have to get done at home or at work.

Money problems can cause high levels of stress and depression. They can cause relationships to break up, people to lose their homes, and families to split up – all of which are additional sources of stress

Loneliness and social isolation

Loneliness and social isolation are major causes of stress, particularly for older people. Loneliness has been shown to affect health and mental wellbeing. People who are lonely are more likely to find everyday experiences more stressful and at the same time they get less support from others to cope with this stress.

> 'I looked after my Mum, who had Parkinson's Disease, for ten years. It was worrying, of course, and sometimes it was difficult to fit everything into a day but I thought I could just take it all in my stride. After Mum died, I had two heart attacks and it was my cardiac rehabilitation nurse, Bev, who taught me not to bottle everything up – to let go and have a good weep – to let all the stress out.
>
> I hadn't realised how much I had been dealing with looking after my mother. Talking to someone, having relaxing hobbies and being active help. I love to walk in the mountains on my holidays – there's nothing like it to blow away your cares.'
>
> *Ina Taylor, 66, Mansfield*

How stressed are you?

We all experience 'stress' in different ways. What one person finds stressful might be an enjoyable challenge to someone else. For each of us, there is 'good stress' as well as 'bad stress' – for example, being under pressure to get something done may motivate you to get it done. However, some experiences – such as being made redundant or being bereaved – can have a negative effect.

Not sure if you're stressed?

When you are exposed to long periods of stress, your body gives you a warning that something is wrong.

BRITISH HEART FOUNDATION

These physical, emotional, behavioural and mental signs should not be ignored. They tell you that you need to slow down. If you continue to be stressed and you don't give your body a break, you may develop health problems.

One in five people in the UK feels 'very' or 'extremely' stressed by their work. Over half say their jobs are getting more stressful and that work is overtaking their home lives

If you think you might be experiencing stress, you need to tune into your early warning signs and think about how you feel, how it shows and how it affects other people.

Check out your warning signs and symptoms of stress

Physical

Do you experience...

- ❑ feeling sweaty or shivery?
- ❑ heart beating fast?
- ❑ dry mouth?
- ❑ headache?
- ❑ loss of appetite for food, fun or sex?
- ❑ weight gain or loss?
- ❑ tight, knotty feelings in your stomach?
- ❑ needing to go to the toilet a lot more than usual?
- ❑ difficulty sleeping, disturbed nights or waking early?
- ❑ tiredness or exhaustion?
- ❑ odd aches and pains?

Emotional

Do you often feel...

- ❑ upset?
- ❑ irritable?
- ❑ tearful?
- ❑ worried?
- ❑ sick in the stomach?
- ❑ isolated from people around you?

Behavioural

Do you...

- ❑ smoke or drink more than you used to?
- ❑ lack a sense of humour?
- ❑ neglect your personal appearance?
- ❑ forget things?
- ❑ work until you're exhausted?
- ❑ clench your jaws or grind your teeth?
- ❑ withdraw from relationships or social situations?
- ❑ start tasks and not finish them?
- ❑ lack concentration?

Mental

Do you think...

- ❑ I can't do this
- ❑ I'll never finish
- ❑ I can't cope – everything is pointless

Many of these signs and symptoms can be associated with general health problems and can be a natural reaction to dealing with short-term problems. Add up how many boxes you ticked.

If you ticked more than four boxes, you may be suffering from prolonged stress.

If you ticked fewer than four boxes, you may not be suffering adversely from stress at the moment.

The quiz below can help you identify how you view your current situation.

Quiz: Am I stressed?

Check your stress levels by ticking the answers below that best describe you.

1. Which of the following best describes how much time you have to do everything you need to do?

- ❑ **A** I have enough time to get everything done.
- ❑ **B** I usually manage to get most things done.
- ❑ **C** I have to prioritise my time very carefully.
- ❑ **D** I always seem to be short of time and rushing to catch up.

2. When you are under a lot of pressure, do you:

- ❑ **A** cope well because it doesn't happen very often?
- ❑ **B** put in more effort so you can get through the difficult patch?
- ❑ **C** give yourself breathing space and time to take stock?
- ❑ **D** drink lots of coffee, and keep going until you're exhausted?

BRITISH HEART FOUNDATION

3. How well do you usually sleep?

- ☐ **A** I sleep really well and feel rested in the morning.
- ☐ **B** I sometimes have trouble falling asleep, but generally get enough sleep.
- ☐ **C** I use relaxation methods and clear my mind before I go to bed.
- ☐ **D** I have frequent restless nights and often wake early.

4. Which of the following best describes the way you deal with difficult situations?

- ☐ **A** I rarely get ruffled about things.
- ☐ **B** I get annoyed a bit more often than I used to.
- ☐ **C** I have a shorter fuse now than I used to, but I think before I react to things.
- ☐ **D** I regularly lose my temper at the smallest things.

5. Which option best describes how much time you have for the things you enjoy?

- ☐ **A** I regularly spend time doing things I enjoy.
- ☐ **B** I have less and less time to do the things I enjoy.
- ☐ **C** Time is tight, but I make sure I have some time each day to relax and enjoy life.
- ☐ **D** I don't have time for hobbies or things I enjoy.

6. Which option best describes how you feel most of the time?

- ☐ **A** I feel fine and able to cope with things.
- ☐ **B** I sometimes get headaches, which are worse when I'm under pressure.
- ☐ **C** I'm under pressure, but I use relaxation methods to make sure I don't get too tense.
- ☐ **D** I often feel tearful and panicky because of the pressure I am under.

Add up how many A, B, C and D answers you gave.

Mostly As It appears from your answers that you are not under a great deal of stress. You have a good balance in your life at the moment. Look out for signs of becoming stressed in the future.

Mostly Bs You seem to be experiencing some stress and are feeling the consequences in various aspects of your life. Try taking positive steps to deal with this stress – for example, by taking regular exercise, making time for yourself, and getting any support you need.

Mostly Cs While you experience some stress, you have developed a range of skills to cope with this. Well done for recognising that stress needs to be dealt with – and for coming up with ways like relaxation and time management to help you to get on with life.

Mostly Ds You seem to be experiencing a lot of stress and this may adversely affect both your physical health and your relationships. Think about how you might start to reduce your stress levels. You could talk to someone about how stress is making you feel.

⇨ The above information is an extract from the British Heart Foundation document *Coping with stress* and is reprinted with permission. Visit the BHF website at www.bhf.org.uk for more information on this and other related topics.

AAAH!
STRESS

BRITISH HEART FOUNDATION

Money worries top Britons' stress lists

Financial angst is the biggest cause of stress for 40% of adults, research shows, with more people aware of the fragility of their jobs as the economy struggles to recover.

Money worries are the main concern of stressed-out Britons, according to the result of a poll published today which reveals that as many as 40 million adults admit to suffering from some form of regular anxiety.

Financial angst is the single biggest cause of stress for 40% of us, followed by problems with friends and family members (25%), health concerns (24%) and stress at work (22%). The recession has caused further headaches with concerns about redundancy or unemployment fifth on the list, cited by 21% of adults surveyed.

The research was carried out by market researchers Mintel. Its senior health analyst, Alexandra Richmond, said: 'Even though the recession may be over, people have become more aware of the fragility of their jobs, or indeed the price of their home, which is why employment and finance top our list of worries.'

Britain's women are revealed as the nation's biggest worriers, with increased numbers of men (55%) more likely than women (45%) to say they are not troubled by anything. More than one in ten (11%) women claims to have five or more worries compared to just one in 14 men.

When it comes to dealing with stress, the British stiff upper lip prevails. As many as 16 million of us talk to family and friends as a way of coping with stress, but only 6% of respondents felt able to turn to a professional for help, such as regular counselling.

And given their serious financial concerns, people are having to find cheaper ways of managing their stress than going on holiday. For 'affordable escapism', an estimated 20 million adults listen to music or read a book to unwind. And controversial complementary medicines – used by two million adults – are popular as an over-the-counter alternative to antidepressants.

Meanwhile, more than one in five of us (21%) admit to turning to drink when stressed, while more than one in ten (13%) light up a cigarette. But men and women have different ways of coping, the research shows. Almost a quarter (24%) of men admit they turn to drink to drown their sorrows, compared with less than one in five (17%) women. By contrast, almost 20% of women turn to comfort foods, snacks and treats in times of trouble compared to just 9% of men.

Richmond said: 'The fact that over half of us turns to our family and friends in times of trouble, compared to just 6% who go to a professional, highlights the extent of the stigma attached to seeking professional help to deal with stress.

'For many, seeking professional help may be regarded as a sign of defeat or inability to cope on their own. It is here that the British "stiff upper lip" syndrome really affects people's ability to get help when things overwhelm them.'

Last week, the strong link between economic downturn and depression was demonstrated when it was revealed the number of suicides in the UK has risen sharply since the recession began, reversing the downward trend of the past decade.

The figures from the Office for National Statistics showed a 6% increase, from 5,377 deaths in 2007 to 5,706 in 2008 among those aged over 15.

3 February 2010

Affordable escapism

THE GUARDIAN

Stress, guilt and exhaustion 'toxic mix' for middle-class parents

Flexible work and more equal parental leave vital for good parenting.

Inflexible, stressful and emotionally demanding jobs can undermine parenting confidence and contribute to emotional withdrawal from children, shows a new report from the think tank Demos. While educational background has little effect on parenting style, work conditions were shown to make an impact.

Although being employed was in general positive for parenting, the kind of work parents did had an impact. Work impacted negatively on parenting when it was characterised by inflexibility – in terms of hours and culture in the workplace. Importantly, parents in well-paid but highly stressful jobs experienced as much negative impact as those in mundane, low-paid and low-skill jobs, because of the lack of choice about working long hours and emotional demands of the workplace. The ability to be creative at work, as well as flexible with hours, had a positive impact on parenting.

Inflexible, stressful and emotionally demanding jobs can undermine parenting confidence and contribute to emotional withdrawal from children, shows a new report from the think tank Demos

Guilt associated with working difficult hours was found to damage parents' self-confidence and confidence in their parenting ability, though the parent's own perception of this was far greater than any impact observed during research. Informal, community support networks were found to improve parental confidence.

Fathers work longer hours than childless men. One in three fathers work more than a 48-hour week, while one in four men without children work more than 48 hours per week. 12 per cent of fathers work more than 60 hours per week. Fathers also increase their working hours once their youngest child is six years old. Fewer men than women use their right to request flexible work. One third of fathers work on flexitime or work from home.

The number of mothers who work has more than tripled from one in six in 1951 to two in three in 2008. Mothers in the UK are now more likely to work than not work. Mothers with partners are more likely to work part-time (41 per cent) over full-time (31 per cent). Lone mothers are just as likely to work full-time as they are part-time (28 and 27 per cent). Six per cent of mothers work a 48-hour week and three per cent work more than 60 hours per week.

New polling found that 41 per cent of fathers were in favour of introducing 'use it or lose it' paternity leave, compared to only 31 per cent of mothers. Overall, 66 per cent of parents were positive or neutral on the issue and only 28 per cent opposed 'use it or lose it' paternity leave. Less than half of mothers surveyed would be happy for their partner to be the main carer, showing that gendered attitudes towards work and care go both ways.

With the number of working parents continuing to rise, and mothers still doing the majority of domestic tasks, Demos recommends the following measures.

- **Boost the capacity of organisations to offer flexible work.** Businesses must be encouraged to support employees who request flexible work. The recession and rise in unemployment should be used as an opportunity to experiment with flexible working arrangements.
- **Encourage shared parenting through an equal system of parental leave.** Parental leave should be on the basis of 'use it or lose it' for both mothers and fathers and include an element of transferable leave.
- **Engage fathers in parenting-related public services.** Health visitors and Sure Start workers should always ask to register both the mother and father of the child. They should receive training on how to appeal to and encourage fathers and male carers as parents.

Kitty Ussher, director of Demos, said:

'Our working lives are inextricably bound up with our home lives and the ability of parents to support their children will be shaped by their freedom to balance care with their responsibilities at work.

'But work does not have a straightforward relationship with parenting. It's not only the number of hours worked, but also the flexibility of a parent's schedule and the quality of their work that makes a difference to children.'

DEMOS

Jen Lexmond, author of the report, said:

'Work has a profound effect on parenting across all incomes. The right kind of work that is flexible and stimulating can improve parenting. But these kinds of jobs often come hand in hand with high levels of stress and emotional exhaustion which can be a toxic mix for parental confidence.

'What's clear is that our jobs make it difficult to share parenting responsibilities – the result too often being a double shift for mothers and a lack of engagement from fathers. We have to recognise that our current system of parental leave and current approach to flexible working is supporting these gendered trends and the result isn't good for anyone – mothers, fathers or children.'

The report also found that parents find their role harder as children got older rather than perfecting 'the art of parenting'. Parents in the research expressed concerns that they became less careful and less effective with their second or third child and many said their confidence levels plunged at the time their children reached adolescence.

Demos recommends a parent refresher class offered when their child starts primary school to help boost parental confidence through this transition period.

The report identifies three key trends that have radically changed the way Britain parents:

- **A stalling of social mobility.** As social mobility has reached a plateau, parenting has become a greater determinant of children's life chances.
- **An atomised society.** As society has become more individualistic, parents may be more isolated and anxious about raising children.
- **A difficult balance of work and care.** As the division of labour has changed at work and at home, parents' roles have become more complex and harder to manage.

Dr Maggie Atkinson, Children's Commissioner for England said:

'The Demos research is a powerful example of how children are at the heart of families, and meeting their needs is key to understanding many of the decisions parents make. Work is one of those important areas where families face difficult decisions over time and money. What we know from this research is that when decisions about flexible working are based on the needs of the child, the family as a whole benefits. The lesson from this is that we have to look at ways of working that allow parents to share responsibility and provide children with the support parents want to give.'

Notes

Demos polled 1,017 parents (560 mothers, 457 fathers) with SurveyShack and iMama.tv. Parents were polled on how they feel about parenting, support services, and the pressures and influences on their lives. iMama.tv is the first video-driven parenting website in the world, hosting over 3,000 custom-made, TV-quality, short videos from both mums and experts, covering everything a parent could want to know about pregnancy, birth and beyond.

The 2009 Demos report *Building Character* detailed how 'tough love' parenting with warmth and consistent boundaries was best at developing crucial character capabilities – empathy, application and self-regulation – that have a significant impact on people's life chances.

The Home Front is the second report on parenting from the Family and Society programme at Demos.

The Home Front employed a mixed research methodology that combined representative attitudinal polling of parents with detailed, micro-level ethnographic observations of family life and parent-child interaction. This primary research has been supplemented with secondary longitudinal data analysis of the British and Millennium Cohort Studies, a literature and policy review, and a series of case studies with parenting services.

The Home Front by Jen Lexmond, Louise Bazalgette and Julia Margo is published on Monday 17 January 2011 and will be available to download for free from www.demos.co.uk

17 January 2011

➪ The above information is reprinted with kind permission from Demos. The study was funded by the Children's Commissioner. Visit www.demos.co.uk for more information.

DEMOS

- control – such as how much say the individual has in the way they do their work;
- support – such as the encouragement, sponsorship and resources provided by the organisation, line management and colleagues. This can also include work-life balance;
- relationships – such as promoting positive working to avoid conflict and dealing with unacceptable behaviour;
- role – such as whether people understand their role within the organisation, and whether the organisation ensures that they do not have conflicting roles;
- change – such as how organisational change, large or small, is managed and communicated within the organisation.

Employers can manage stress in the workplace by taking steps to reduce the risk of their employees experiencing stress in the first place and by supporting those who do encounter stress

Assessing stress risks

Employers have a duty to ensure that risks arising from work activity are properly controlled. The Management Standards approach helps employers work with their employees and representatives to undertake a risk assessment for stress. Unlike the risk assessment for physical hazards, it is likely that the risk assessment on stress will be carried out at a departmental or organisational level.

Identifying contributory factors

The factors that contribute to occupational stress can be identified by using existing information to see how your organisation measures up. This data includes looking at your sickness absence rates, lateness, disciplinary problems or staff turnover. Information can also be obtained from any staff surveys that have been carried out.

Stress audits

Carrying out a stress audit is one of the best ways to find out if stress is a problem within your workplace. A stress audit involves talking to staff – either individually or in groups – to find out where there may be problems.

Work Positive

Work Positive is a stress risk management resource, a step-by-step process that assists managers and employers to identify and reduce the potential causes of stress.

Work Positive supports continuous improvement against HSE's Management Standards for Work-related Stress. Work Positive has been redeveloped and updated to allow organisations to continue to conduct this comprehensive assessment of the known causes of stress, as well as easily assess their performance against the HSE Standards.

Work Positive was originally developed by NHS Health Scotland and the Health and Safety Authority (HSA, Ireland) to help organisations identify the potential causes of stress at work in line with requirements under the Management of Health and Safety at Work Regulations 1999.

Work Positive is a comprehensive risk-management process that incorporates a risk assessment covering the known causes of workplace stress.

Good practices around occupational stress

Employers can manage stress in the workplace by taking steps to reduce the risk of their employees experiencing stress in the first place and by supporting those who do encounter stress.

Meanwhile, individuals can act on a personal level within their sphere of influence in the home and work environments to reduce sources of stress and to combat its effects.

Not all employers will have the time or resources to introduce all the examples listed below, especially in small organisations.

However, the principles of how to control and manage stress still apply and all employers have a legal obligation to take work-related stress seriously.

Self-help for stress

Individuals can do a great deal to manage stress for themselves. Effective measures include regular exercise, sensible eating, adequate sleep and avoiding the use of alcohol, tobacco and drugs.

Individuals should also learn to recognise signs of stress, how to practise relaxation techniques and when to seek professional help.

Individuals are more willing to admit that they are suffering from stress – a vital first step to tackling it – if they can expect to be dealt with sympathetically.

Assisting self-help for stress

Employers can provide regular in-house training events or encourage staff to attend stress management training events that are available locally.

Other assistances can include access to leisure facilities for exercise at a reduced cost or free or reduced cost relaxation therapies such as head or neck massage sessions.

A calendar of events for complementary treatments and regular social events at lunch times can also help combat stress and keep up awareness of the benefits of such activities.

Training in stress awareness and management

Managers and supervisors should be trained to help individuals cope with stress and to recognise when expert help is needed.

Individuals can benefit from training in stress management techniques.

Workplace stress policies

Employers may want to think about introducing a stress policy for the workplace.

The policy should provide clear guidelines for managing stress in the work environment and should:

- recognise stress at work as a health and safety problem
- detail arrangements for accessing counselling
- formalise arrangements for assessing the causes of stress in the workplace
- introduce measures to reduce and prevent stress
- detail arrangements for employees suffering as the results of stress.

Employee Assistance Programmes

Some organisations operate Employee Assistance Programmes (EAPs). These are confidential personal counselling services sponsored, and usually paid for, by employers.

Estimated days (full-day equivalent) lost from work due to a self-reported work-related illness or workplace injury (central figures), 2009/10

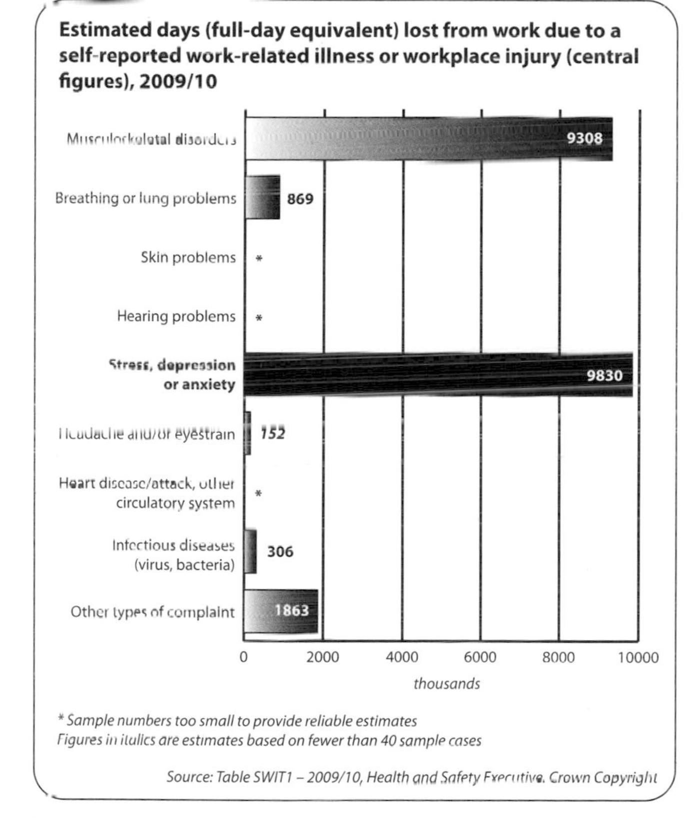

** Sample numbers too small to provide reliable estimates*
Figures in italics are estimates based on fewer than 40 sample cases

Source: Table SWIT1 – 2009/10, Health and Safety Executive. Crown Copyright

Typically, EAPs provide professional counsellors to discuss with individuals their work or non-work-related problems. Such problems may be emotional, financial or legal, and may be linked to alcohol or drug misuse, etc.

EAPs can be run in-house, wholly contracted out to counselling organisations, or managed from within the organisation using external counsellors.

⇨ Reproduced with kind permission from the Scottish Centre for Healthy Working Lives, published by NHS Health Scotland (www.healthyworkinglives.com and www.healthscotland.com), April 2011.

Summary of the law on stress at work

Stress means different things to different people, but in general terms it's a reaction to excessive pressure or harassment at work. This article is solely concerned with stress in the workplace.

What do workers have to prove?

In a stress case, workers first have to prove that they have a psychiatric illness (the injury). Then they have to show:

- That their employer breached their duty of care.
- That their working environment posed a real risk of causing the illness and the employer knew (or ought to have known) that they were exposed to that risk. Workers then have to prove that their employer knew that the difficulties they faced were so severe as to create a risk of an imminent psychiatric illness. In order to prove this 'foreseeability', claimants often have to produce a report from a doctor or prove that they have been off work before due to a similar illness.
- That their employer failed in their duty of care towards them. This involves showing that the employer did not do everything that was reasonable in the circumstances to keep the worker safe from harm. This includes the court looking at how the employer dealt with any risks.
- That the harm they suffered was caused by their working environment and their employer's breach of the duty of care owed to them.

Was it foreseeable?

Proving that the psychiatric injury was foreseeable by the employer is a crucial part of any stress at work claim. It is very difficult to prove. The courts have said that foreseeability depends on what the employer knew or ought to have known about the pressure on the individual employee at the time. That doesn't mean employers have to ask about a worker's state of health all the time, but if there are obvious things happening (for instance, the person keeps bursting into tears), then the House of Lords has said that they would expect a reasonable employer to realise that there might be a problem. Take the 1995 landmark case of Walker v Northumberland County Council, in which Mr Walker had two nervous breakdowns. As the employer had been deemed to have been 'put on notice' after the first breakdown, Mr Walker's second breakdown was therefore entirely foreseeable as they did not provide the extra help they promised him. However, since then, there have been a number of notable cases (such as Hatton v Sutherland and Barber v Somerset County Council) which have made clear the extent of the onus on claimants to prove their claim.

Once an employer has become aware that a worker seems to be struggling, they must investigate the problem and find out what they can do to resolve it. This will depend, to some extent, on the size of the employer and the resources available to them. In particular, the courts have said that an employer who offers a confidential counselling advice service is unlikely to be in breach of their duty. That does not mean, however, they are a 'panacea' in all cases and just having a counselling service is not enough to correct an employer's breach of duty of care.

Who was to blame?

Workers also have to show that it was more likely than not that their employer was to blame as a result of a breach of their duty. This is called the 'balance of probabilities'. Claimants can prove that they were at fault either by showing that their employer breached a 'common law duty' (law made by judges) or a statutory duty (an actual law).

What does the law say?

The common law says that employers are responsible for the general safety of their employees while they are at work. In addition, employers have to comply with a number of statutes, such as:

- The Health and Safety at Work Act 1974 which states that employers have a duty to ensure that, as far as is reasonably practicable, their workplaces are safe and healthy. They also have to take measures to control any risks that they identify.
- The Management of Health and Safety at Work Regulations 1999 state that employers must carry out a risk assessment of the risks in the workplace. Any measures they take to control the risks must be based on this assessment.

Employees can also rely on the following statutes if they want to bring a claim of stress at work, depending on the circumstances:

- Disability Discrimination Act 1995 – stress may turn out to be the sign of an underlying condition that would amount to a disability. Under the Act, employers are required to make reasonable adjustments to the

THOMPSONS SOLICITORS LLP

workplace, such as reducing the employee's workload or pressures on an employee who is under stress.

- Discrimination legislation – if someone is being treated unfairly by, say, a line manager who treats female staff in an overbearing and dominating way, they may be able to argue that such behaviour amounts to sex discrimination.

What about the Protection from Harassment Act?

As a result of two decisions in 2006, it seemed that the Protection from Harassment Act (PHA) 1997 offered a good route for potential claimants suffering from stress. In Majrowski v Guy's and St Thomas's NHS Trust, the House of Lords said that employees could use the PHA to sue their employers for damages for workplace harassment. Likewise, the High Court in Green v DB Group Services (UK) Ltd said that employers could be liable for the same acts of bullying resulting in psychiatric injury under both the common law and the PHA. However, in most cases it is far from easy to prove that an employer was liable under the PHA. To fall within it, the conduct complained about must:

- Have occurred on more than one occasion.
- Be targeted at the claimant and intended to cause distress.
- Be serious enough to amount to a criminal act (according to the Court of Appeal in the 2008 case of Conn v Sunderland City Council. The Court confirmed that the nature of the bullying throughout the course of conduct had to be of such severity that criminal proceedings could be pursued under section 2 of the Act).
- Not simply amount to a disagreement between two work colleagues.
- Represent an intense connection between the conduct and the job of work.
- Not be considered to be reasonable and proper criticism of poor performance.

Thompsons' website includes regular legal updates in the e-training section of the website. The information contained in this article is not a substitute for legal advice. You should talk to a lawyer or adviser before making a decision about what to do. Thompsons Solicitors is a trading name of Thompsons Solicitors LLP and is regulated by the Solicitors Regulation Authority.

Published May 2010

- Information from Thompsons Solicitors LLP. Visit www.thompsons.law.co.uk for more information.

Common causes of stress at work

It's important to recognise the common causes of stress at work so that you can take steps to reduce stress levels where possible.

Some typical stress inducers

- Excessively high workloads, with unrealistic deadlines making people feel rushed, under pressure and overwhelmed.
- Insufficient workloads, making people feel that their skills are being under-used.
- A lack of control over work activities.
- A lack of interpersonal support or poor working relationships leading to a sense of isolation.
- People being asked to do a job for which they have insufficient experience or training.
- Difficulty settling into a new promotion, both in terms of meeting the new role's requirements and adapting to possible changes in relationships with colleagues.
- Concerns about job security, lack of career opportunities, or level of pay.
- Bullying or harassment.
- A blame culture within your business where people are afraid to get things wrong or to admit to making mistakes.
- Weak or ineffective management which leaves employees feeling they don't have a sense of direction, or over-management, which can leave employees feeling undervalued and affect their self-esteem.
- Multiple reporting lines for employees, with each manager asking for their work to be prioritised.
- Failure to keep employees informed about significant changes to the business, causing them uncertainty about their future.
- A poor physical working environment, e.g. excessive heat, cold or noise, inadequate lighting, uncomfortable seating, malfunctioning equipment, etc.

- The above information is reprinted with kind permission from Business Link. Visit www.businesslink.gov.uk for more information.

Stressed out? It could be in your genes

To their surprise, neuroscientists have discovered that stress can be passed down the generations – and even though it can be harmful, there is a logical biological reason.

By Laura Spinney

Stress: there's not a system in your body it doesn't poison in the end. Over time, it raises your blood pressure, increases your chances of infertility and makes you age faster, and that's not all. Remove the source of the stress and all those horrors vanish, right?

Wrong. A growing body of scientific evidence suggests that not only can stress bring about permanent changes in your body, but you can even pass on some of those changes to your offspring. What's more, some researchers are now arguing that, far from being an exclusively human problem, psychological stress is rampant in nature. Its influence is so powerful, they claim, that like the conductor of an orchestra, it imposes a rhythm on whole ecosystems, determining which species are booming, and which are bust.

In fact, says Rachel Yehuda, a neuroscientist at the Mount Sinai School of Medicine in New York City, it's time to rewrite the textbooks about stress, doing away with the outdated idea that its effects are transient. 'Some effects of the environment and of experience are long lasting,' she says. 'And for that we need a new biology.' Yehuda had her first inkling of the indelible mark that stress can leave on families back in 1993, when she opened a clinic to treat the psychological problems of Holocaust survivors, and was deluged with calls from their adult children. Investigating further, she found that those children were particularly prone to post-traumatic stress disorder (PTSD). Both parents and children tended to have low levels of the hormone cortisol in their urine. Stranger still, the more severe the Holocaust survivor's PTSD symptoms, the less cortisol there was in their child's urine.

Cortisol plays an important role in the body's stress response. When a threat presents itself, the brain instructs the adrenal glands, just above the kidneys, to release hormones, including adrenaline, into the blood. The result is the racing heart, rapid breathing and so on that prepare us for fight or flight. When the threat has passed, the brain sends another signal to the adrenal glands to release cortisol. Cortisol shuts down the stress response by binding to receptors in certain regions of the brain, including the hippocampus.

At McGill University in Montreal, Canada, neuroscientist Michael Meaney has shown that stressful events in the early lives of rats, such as being reared by a negligent mother, can affect their response to stress as adults. The pups of negligent mothers grow up to be fearful and skittish, and they have fewer hippocampal receptors to corticosterone (the rat equivalent of cortisol) than the pups of attentive mothers.

Last year, Meaney's group made headlines when it reported a similar finding in humans. Meaney's former student Patrick McGowan managed to get hold of tissue samples from the brains of 24 adults who had committed suicide, half of whom had been abused as children, and half of whom had not. The researchers found that the hippocampi of the abuse victims contained fewer cortisol receptors than those of the individuals who had not been abused.

A growing body of scientific evidence suggests that not only can stress bring about permanent changes in your body, but you can even pass on some of those changes to your offspring

In both rats and humans, therefore, stressful early life events leave an enduring trace in the brain, causing those brains to be less sensitive to the stress-dampening effects of cortisol. And in both species, that reduced sensitivity is associated with so-called epigenetic changes – chemical modifications to DNA that alter the activity of genes without altering the genes themselves. Genetic change, also known as evolution, takes millions of years, but epigenetic changes can be accumulated in a lifetime, allowing organisms to adapt more quickly than their genomes can. Or as biochemist Susan Gasser of the Friedrich Miescher Institute for Biomedical Research in Basel, Switzerland, puts it: 'Epigenetics frees us from being a prisoner of our genes.'

Meaney's group found that the gene encoding the corticosterone receptor in rats carries different epigenetic marks, or modifications, in the brains of the offspring of negligent and attentive mothers.

As a result, the gene is less active in the neglected offspring, meaning that it is translated into fewer of those critical receptors – the ones responsible for shutting down the stress response – with profound consequences for the pups' behaviour. They found a similar difference between the abused and the non-abused suicide victims.

Yehuda began to wonder if epigenetic mechanisms could explain the vulnerability to PTSD of the children of Holocaust survivors. This is a radical proposal, since

THE INDEPENDENT

it implies that epigenetic changes can be transmitted from one generation to the next. Most epigenetic marks are erased during the formation of the gametes – the sperm and egg – so that each generation starts out a blank slate. However, there is now good evidence that some survive that erasure process, and stress-related marks are among them.

Why should the effects of stress be so robust? Do they represent a failure of the system whereby our epigenetic status is reset to zero at conception, or could offspring that are programmed by their mothers for life in a dog-eat-dog world – offspring that are fearful, jittery, or in the jargon of psychiatrists, 'hypervigilant' – actually have a better chance of survival than their more-relaxed counterparts?

It's a counter intuitive idea, but studies in animals other than humans suggest there might be some truth in it. In European starlings, for example, a female's stress hormones contaminate the yolk of her eggs, meaning that her young are exposed to them from the earliest stages of life. Oliver Love, a behavioural ecologist at the University of Windsor in Ontario, Canada, has shown that fledglings that were exposed to high levels of stress hormones in the egg perform better in flight trials than fledglings that were not, because their wing muscles mature earlier. '[Stress] prepares them better for escape from predators,' Love says. Rudy Boonstra of the University of Toronto's Centre for the Neurobiology of Stress, thinks that this kind of heritable stress response could explain the dynamics of entire food chains. In the boreal forest that covers half of Canada, for example, a suite of predators that includes lynx, coyotes and great horned owls prey on the snowshoe hare. 300 years ago, fur traders who in turn preyed on lynx had already noticed a strange relationship between predator and prey. The hare population cycles from low to high to low again, reaching its highest density approximately once a decade. Lynx numbers follow suit, with a lag of one or two years.

After 30 years of probing this mysterious synchrony, Boonstra thinks he has finally got to the bottom of it. When hare numbers are low and its predators numerous, hare mothers are stressed – not surprisingly, since hare mortality is close to 95 per cent at this point in the cycle – and the researchers can read the hormonal signature of that stress in the high cortisol content of their faeces. 'We know what the hares are thinking, in the endocrinological sense,' explains Boonstra.

He thinks that the hare mothers pass on that stress signature to their offspring, which then grow up to be hypervigilant. As in the case of Love's sparrows, that might prepare them to better evade their predators, so that they have a better chance of surviving and reproducing. Meanwhile, finding food becomes harder for the lynx, whose numbers continue to fall, only entering the upswing of recovery once hare numbers have recovered to a certain extent themselves, and the juveniles have become less wary again.

McGowan is now working with Boonstra to investigate the epigenetic mechanisms that might underpin that waxing and waning of wariness in the hares. Boonstra predicts that they will find big differences in the numbers of cortisol receptors in the brains of juveniles at the peaks and troughs of the cycle. 'Predators are amazingly important in structuring communities,' he says. 'Until now we've focused on the direct effects of predators, but the indirect effects, the psychological effects, may be as great or greater.'

What can such findings tell us about humans? Yehuda's work strongly suggests that a modified stress response may be heritable in us too. However, there is one major difference between people and the animals in Canada's boreal forest: we are long-lived.

Human longevity means that, unlike a hare, a person is unlikely to inhabit the same environment that her parents did, which in turn means that there is a risk of a mismatch between the environment she was programmed for, and the one she enters. It's that mismatch that can cause problems. As Yehuda points out, hypervigilance might be a boon for a prisoner in a concentration camp, but in a modern city in peacetime it can be a serious handicap – as she found when she began to treat the children of Holocaust survivors for PTSD.

We live long partly because we have been so successful in shaping our own environment. When it comes to stress, therefore, we may be the victims of our own success.

2 December 2010

THE INDEPENDENT

Chapter 3

LEARNING TO COPE

What can you do about stress?

There are a number of ways to tackle stress in your life. Think about whether you can do any of the following.

Avoid the sources of your stress

Once you have pinpointed the main sources of stress in your life, think about what you could do to avoid them. For example:

- If traffic jams are causing you stress, think about how you can change your journey to work. For example, can you leave earlier or later, or can you walk, cycle or use public transport part or all of the way, or take a different route to work?
- If your workload is too great, talk to your manager and ask if you can have extra help, attend a time management course or have some extra training.
- If you are having family problems, talk things through with those close to you. Plan to have some time enjoying things together. Or think about having some counselling.
- If you are just too busy, prioritise and drop some of your commitments.

Change how you respond to stressful situations

If you can't remove the source of your stress, try to focus on changing your attitude towards it. Think about how you respond both physically and mentally when you are in a stressful situation.

Physical response

When you are stressed, you may get physical symptoms such as tense muscles, taking short, fast breaths, or feeling butterflies in your stomach. Instead, take some slow, deep breaths, or try some relaxation techniques (see page 34), and remind yourself that getting stressed won't help the situation.

Mental response

When pressure mounts up, it's easy to become defensive, frustrated, angry or depressed. If you start to feel that you're getting stressed, take a step back. Give yourself some space, take some time and plan what you can do to ease the situation.

If you have negative thoughts going through your mind – like 'I can't cope', or 'I'm useless' – try challenging them with more positive thoughts, such as, 'I know I will get through this in time' or 'There are lots of things I am good at and valued for'.

If you can't remove the source of your stress, try to focus on changing your attitude towards it. Think about how you respond both physically and mentally when you are in a stressful situation

'As a university lecturer I did feel the pressure to perform, especially in front of large audiences, which could be quite stressful. And the work and the travel left me too tired to do any exercise. Now I work from home it's much better, but there are still stresses and strains – especially if my baby son's being very demanding when I'm trying to work.

I find going to the gym's great for de-stressing, and yoga helps me relax so I try to make sure it's part of my daily/weekly routine. It can be all too easy to make an excuse not to leave the house! Peace and quiet's important too – you need to learn to enjoy yourself, take things a bit easier, and enjoy the present.'

Haider Ali, 43, North London

Make changes to your lifestyle to help reduce the effects of stress on your body

Top healthy lifestyle tips to tackle stress:

- Eat well
- Keep physically active
- Keep alcohol to within healthy limits
- Don't smoke
- Learn to relax

BRITISH HEART FOUNDATION

- Make time for rest
- Manage your time
- Seek help and get support.

Eat well

Your body is able to fight stressful situations better when you take the time to eat well. Try to:

- eat regular meals
- eat a wide variety of healthy foods
- have at least five portions of fruit and vegetables a day
- make sure that at least one-third of your food comes from bread, pasta, beans, rice, potatoes or pulses
- choose foods low in saturated fat
- cut down on salt and sugar
- have less tea, coffee and other drinks with caffeine, and drink plenty of water
- reach a healthy weight and maintain it, and
- combine healthy eating habits with a regular physical activity programme.

For more on healthy eating, see the British Heart Foundation booklet *Eating well*, available on their website (www.bhf.org.uk).

...THINK I'M LEAVING STRESS BEHIND!

Keep physically active

Moderate-intensity physical activity (activity that gets you warm and slightly out of breath) has been shown to release endorphins – natural substances that help you feel better and maintain a positive attitude. Doing regular physical activity for 30 minutes a day on at least five days a week will help you cope with stress.

It will also:

- lower your risk of coronary heart disease, diabetes and stroke;
- provide you with more energy and stamina;
- help to you to maintain a healthy weight; and
- help to reduce the risk of some cancers.

The 30 minutes can be split into smaller time slots of at least ten minutes at a time.

Choose activities that you enjoy and set yourself realistic reasonable goals. Or choose different activities each day to keep you interested and motivated. Even a brisk half-hour walk every day can make a difference to how you feel, look and cope with life.

If you have high blood pressure or get angina, or if you have another medical condition, you should talk to your GP before suddenly increasing your activity levels or taking up any new activity.

Keep alcohol to within healthy limits

When you feel stressed, you might be tempted to look for easy solutions such as the relaxed feeling you may get from alcohol. But drinking too much can be harmful for your heart and your health.

Men should not regularly drink more than three to four units in a day. Women should not regularly drink more than two to three units in a day.

One unit of alcohol =

- a small glass (100ml) of wine (10% ABV [alcohol by volume]); or
- half a pint (about 300ml) of normal-strength lager, cider or beer (for example, 3.5% ABV); or
- a pub measure (25ml) of spirits.

Don't smoke

If you smoke, stopping smoking is the single most important thing you can do to improve your heart health, and your general health too.

If you have already tried to quit smoking but have started again, ask your doctor or pharmacist about the stop-smoking aids now available. Getting professional help can increase your chance of success.

BRITISH HEART FOUNDATION

Learn to relax

Learning how to relax is a very good way to cope with stress of any kind, and can promote a feeling of wellbeing. It also reduces anxiety, irritability, and pain caused by tense muscles such as neck ache, back ache and headache.

Once you are practised at doing it, you will find it makes a noticeable difference to your mood and to your energy – not just when you are stressed, but also at other times. It can also have a protective effect on your mental wellbeing – helping to prevent some common mental health problems.

Relaxation is more than just sitting back and being quiet. It is an active process involving techniques that calm your body and mind. Finding relaxation activities that help you unwind and fitting them into your daily life will actually give you more energy and make you more effective at the things you have to get done.

The quick relaxation routine

1. Tune into your breathing. Take one deep breath in, hold it, and then tell yourself to let go as you breathe out through your mouth. Breathe naturally for a while, and then repeat the deep breath and 'letting go' with your outward breath.
2. Tense up and then relax a single muscle group such as your hand, your foot or stomach. When you let go, try to let all the unnecessary tension slip away. Do the same for some other muscle groups.
3. Drop your shoulders.
4. Apply your relaxation skills in increasingly testing situations. You will soon begin to benefit.

You could combine relaxation exercises with your favourite music. Choose something that lifts your mood or that you find soothing. Some people find it easier to relax while listening to specially designed relaxation audio tapes, which provide music and relaxation instructions. You can download and listen to a range of podcasts from the Mental Health Foundation to help you relax (see www.mentalhealth.org.uk/information/wellbeing-podcasts).

Other popular ways to relax include yoga, pilates and meditation. You could join a local class for one of these, or practise at home. Once you find a relaxation method that works for you, practise it every day for at least 30 minutes.

Make time for rest

Even with a healthy diet and exercise, you can't fight stress effectively without rest. You need time to recover from exertion and stressful events.

Make enough time to relax your mind as well as your body. It could be sitting down with the newspaper, going for a short walk, or having a cup of tea with a friend. Some people find that switching off and taking a nap during the day helps reduce their stress.

Manage your time

For many of us, life is filled with too many demands and too little time. For the most part, over-ambitious goals are ones we have chosen ourselves. This drive to juggle too much means we lose out on time for ourselves. It helps to learn how to manage your time well.

Effective time-management skills involve setting priorities, asking for help when appropriate, pacing yourself and taking time out for yourself.

Seek help and get support

If you feel that things are getting on top of you, try talking about it. Whatever is causing you stress, you can do a lot to help yourself by talking it through with your family or friends. They may be able to 'stand back' from the situation and together you can identify things that will help.

It is better to ask for help rather than struggling on pretending to be able to cope. Speak to someone you trust about the things that are causing you stress. There is support available – use it.

Plan your stress-busting activities for the week

You need to build some 'stress-busting activities' into your day, your week, and your life.

- Think about the week ahead.
- Think through the commitments that you have and the likely 'danger spots' for stressful situations (such as a difficult meeting at work, or a child's birthday party).
- Now plan the stress-busting activities that you are going to build into your week. Go through the list below and choose which ones you will include as part of your plan to de-stress.

Stress-busting activities

Work

If work is stressing you out:

- talk to your manager and together make some changes.
- seek advice from your human resources department.
- talk to a colleague or friend.

Relaxation

You can do this by:

- sitting down and taking some deep breaths.
- doing a series of stretches.
- taking up a new hobby or activity.
- practising yoga, pilates or meditation.

Problem-solving

Ask yourself:

- What is the real problem?
- What can I do differently?
- Reflect on the outcome. Did doing things differently work?
- If it didn't work, try another action plan.

Time management

- Prioritise tasks and plan your day accordingly.
- Do one thing at a time.
- Have realistic short-term and long-term strategies for getting things done.
- Learn to say 'No'. At work, at home and with friends, you sometimes need to put yourself first. Remember to be assertive. Being assertive allows you to stand up for your rights and beliefs while respecting those of others.
- Be realistic about what you can achieve, know your own limits, and celebrate success at every opportunity.
- If you feel overwhelmed, talk about it with a friend, partner or manager.

Some of these changes can take time to develop. Don't expect to be able to change everything at once or to get it 'right' first time. Expecting too much of yourself will possibly add more stress. Be kind to yourself.

The stress chain

This shows you some examples of ways to cope with stress, and how to react more positively to stressful situations.

When you are feeling stressed	What you can do
Be aware of it	• Keep a stress diary • Make a 'hassle list' – a list of all the things that cause you stress • Look out for early warning signs of stress
Reduce the chance of it happening again	• Manage your time • Say 'No' sometimes • Avoid your stress hot spots where possible • Get help and support
Change how you think or feel about stress	• Get the balance right in your life • Take a positive approach • Accept what you can't change
Change how you react to it	• Communicate with our partner and others • Be assertive about your needs • Keep things in perspective • Use relaxation skills like deep breathing • Use humour
Reduce the effects of stress on your body	• Eat well • Be physically active • Have a massage • Relax

Source: Coping with stress, *British Heart Foundation*

The benefits of stress-busting activities

Building some stress-busting activities into your week will mean that:

- you protect yourself from health problems associated with stress;
- you are more efficient at getting things done;
- you have more time for the things you enjoy;
- you enjoy better relationships with family, friends and work colleagues; and
- you feel much better.

Action points

- Avoid sources of stress if you can.
- If you feel stress coming on, take a step back, breathe deeply and take stock.
- Keep things in perspective.
- Make sure you get regular, healthy meals, and cut down on comfort food if it is unhealthy.
- Get plenty of exercise – whatever you enjoy doing.
- Limit alcohol to recommended levels.
- Make sure you have plenty of rest and relaxation.
- Manage your time by prioritising and learning to say 'No'.
- Talk to someone about your feelings if you are finding things difficult.
- Get the help and support you need.

➪ The above information is an extract from the British Heart Foundation document *Coping with stress* and is reprinted with permission. Visit www.bhf.org.uk for more information.

British approach to dealing with stress runs risk of serious mental health problems

Eating junk food, spending time alone or 'just living with it' are the most common approaches to dealing with stress, despite the mental health risks.

Other highlights from the survey:

- One in five people feel stressed every day, with half feeling stressed at least once a week.
- Economic climate reflected as money and work are revealed to be the main causes of stress in Britain.
- Under-25s are the most stressed age group overall and the most stressed about unemployment.
- Liverpool and Milton Keynes are the most stressed cities, Bristol the least.
- Women are more stressed than men about family issues and the laziness of partners, while men are more stressed about work and being single.
- Younger people get most stressed about Christmas and other family gatherings.

To coincide with National Stress Awareness Day, the charity the Mental Health Foundation has published the results of its 'Be Mindful Stress Survey' into the most common causes of, and methods of dealing with, stress across Britain.

When provided with a definition of stress and list of its symptoms, half of all respondents revealed that they feel stressed at least once a week

The survey was conducted as part of the Foundation's ongoing 'Be Mindful' campaign to raise awareness of mindfulness as a clinically-proven way of dealing with stress, following their launch of the UK's first online course in mindfulness, Be Mindful, in September.

When provided with a definition of stress and list of its symptoms, half of all respondents revealed that they feel stressed at least once a week, with one in five (21%) feeling stressed every day. Money-related issues, such as debt or being unable to pay for essentials like food or rent, were given as the main cause of stress for 28% of Britons – the biggest single cause. Work-related issues, such as the threat of redundancies or having too much work to do, were the second most common cause (27%), reflecting recent Health and Safety Executive figures indicating a rise in sick days taken due to work-related stress over recent years. Family and children also registered highly as causes of stress (19%), as did personal relationships (12%).

Mental health risks

Perhaps the most concerning figures in the survey related to how we manage our stress. When asked how they deal with their stress, almost two-thirds of respondents (63%) said that they would do nothing and just live with it, a figure that remained broadly consistent whether people felt stressed every day or less frequently. Nearly a third (30%) said they spend time alone, making it the second most common approach to dealing with stress. The third most common response was to eat comfort or junk food (26%), a response that was particularly common amongst women (33% compared to 18% of men). All three responses are in contrast to recommended stress-

MENTAL HEALTH FOUNDATION

management practice, which advises that people should take steps to manage their stress, remain sociable and talk about their problems, and eat healthily. Without managing it appropriately, stress can result in more serious mental health problems, such as depression, as well as contributing to the risk of physical health problems such as stroke or heart attack.

Healthier approaches to dealing with stress featured further down the list of responses, with discussing it with a friend or family member fourth (24%), taking physical exercise fifth (14%), and practising mindfulness or meditation eighth (6%). Another less healthy method of stress-management – drinking alcohol or taking drugs – was sixth (13%), while taking it out on friends or family was seventh (12%). An indication of the direct way in which unmanaged stress can impact on the economy was in the 3% who responded that they take a day off work when feeling stressed.

Dr Andrew McCulloch, Chief Executive of the Mental Health Foundation, said:

'The economic costs of unmanaged stress are huge and increasing – 11 million lost working days a year at the last count – while the personal costs for those who experience it, and their families and friends, is of equal concern. Unmanaged stress can additionally develop into mental health problems, such as depression, as well as increasing the risk of physical problems such as heart disease.

'The results of the Be Mindful survey suggest that too many of us aren't managing our stress in a healthy way, meaning the drive to raise awareness of mindfulness as a healthy, practical way of managing stress has never been more important. Fortunately, there are a range of excellent books and courses in mindfulness available for people who wish to take control of their own stress management, including our specially developed online course, launched recently for those who might lack the time, money or access to tuition in their area to attend a course.

'Despite the uncertain times ahead, if more people can learn to manage their stress through healthy approaches such as eating well, taking regular exercise, and practising mindfulness, there is no reason why the burden of stress on society need continue as it has been.'

Dr Jonty Heaversedge, South London GP, BBC Street Doctor and co-author of *The Mindful Manifesto*, said:

'Stress is becoming increasingly common in these troubled economic times, and a problem I am seeing more and more amongst my patients. The clinical evidence for mindfulness as an effective method of stress reduction is compelling and, like eating well and taking regular exercise, it is a healthy way in which people can manage their stress so that it doesn't end up taking over their lives or developing into a more serious mental illness.'

3 November 2010

⇨ The above information is reprinted with kind permission from the Mental Health Foundation. Visit www.mentalhealth.org.uk for more information.

Anxiety eased by exercise

A study has shown that people who were regularly active in their spare time had less likelihood of being depressed and anxious.

The study was a joint effort between the Institute of Psychiatry at King's College London and researchers from the Norwegian Institute of Public Health and the University of Bergen in Norway.

The researchers looked at data from 40,000 Norwegian people. They asked the participants how regularly and strenuously they exercised in their free time and during their work hours.

Participants were also assessed using the Hospital Anxiety and Depression Scale.

They saw that people who did not take exercise in their free time had nearly double the likelihood of depression symptoms when compared to people who took the most exercise.

Lead researcher Dr Samuel Harvey, from the Institute of Psychiatry, said: 'Our study shows that people who engage in regular leisure-time activity of any intensity are less likely to have symptoms of depression.

'We also found that the context in which activity takes place is vital and that the social benefits associated with exercise, like increased numbers of friends and social support, are more important in understanding how exercise may be linked to improved mental health than any biological markers of fitness,' he added.

1 November 2010

⇨ The above information is reprinted with kind permission from hc2d.co.uk.

How to cope with the stress of student life

Student life is exciting. But it can also be very pressured and stressful. A lot has to be achieved in the limited time available. This article is aimed at students and their families. It focuses on some of the anxieties that they are likely to encounter as student life begins, and suggests ways of coping.

'So this was how it was, face to face with the future – being alone, having no-one to talk to, being afraid of the city and training college and teaching, and having to pretend that I was not alone, that I had many people to talk to, that I felt at home... and that teaching was what I had longed to do all my life.'

What difficulties should I expect?

Student life is a transitional period. You do a course because you think it will enable you to do or have something that you want, such as increased job opportunities or enhanced enjoyment of life. Studying is part of a process of change and, sometimes, change can cause a lot of anxiety.

Leaving home

If you go to university straight from school, you are facing the challenge of leaving home, separating from your parents and beginning the process of finding your identity, as an adult, and your place in the world. This is a big psychological upheaval. It also involves many challenges at a practical level. You will need to practise housekeeping, manage a budget and find your way around a strange place. This all demands energy, just as you are beginning to take on the work requirements of your course and build a new social life.

Mature students

If you are a mature student you may already have left home, but will still have many changes to deal with. You may have less money to spend, less free time, and experience a change in your social status, for better or worse. You may have a partner and children; your new life will have an impact on them, and your relationship with them will be affected.

Changing identity

When you become a student you may feel differently about yourself, and other people may react to you differently. You will be making new friends, and have a chance to make a fresh start. You may be working with peers who are your intellectual equals, for the first time in your life. You may find you are cleverer than you thought – or not so clever! It takes time to adjust to this new sense of who you are.

MIND

New opportunities

There may be sports, social and political activities open to you now, which you've never tried before. This has two aspects: it can be very exciting, but it can also be terrifying. It can be easy to take on too many things, because you don't want to miss out on any new opportunities. But it would be unwise to go on your first pot-holing expedition, for example, on the same weekend that you are moving into new lodgings and handing in your first essay. Recognise how much you are dealing with at once, and go at your own pace. Be prepared to feel terrified sometimes.

Family relationships

Relationships with your family will change too. This can be especially difficult if you are the first one ever to go to college, or the first of your gender. Other family members can have complicated feelings about this. They may secretly envy you, or be afraid that your new experience will change you too much and make you no longer 'one of us'. Their reactions may cause you to feel insecure, lacking in confidence or guilty about having this opportunity.

Studying is part of a process of change and, sometimes, change can cause a lot of anxiety

But there can also be problems if everyone in the family has been to college. Can you live up to their standards? Do you have to work in the same field as them, or do they feel threatened by your choice of subject? Could they be concerned that you could, in fact, be too successful?

The most important thing with family situations of this kind is that these feelings need to be acknowledged, by being talked about. Only then can everyone involved move towards creating a more supportive environment.

How will I deal with practical issues?

Accommodation, finance, food and travel can all present daunting problems in your first weeks. Ask for help from older students, from other first-years, or from your teachers. Don't be proud – you are not alone in your difficulties.

Most places of education should have sources of advice and information: an accommodation office, to help you find somewhere to live; a financial advice service; and a student advisory service to give other kinds of information. There should also be a students' union. The students' union will often publish a handbook or a welfare manual outlining sources of help.

Eat well

It's very important to eat properly, and not to exist on snacks, beer and coffee: the right foods can help your concentration for studying and help you feel well generally. However, if you are anxious, preparing your own food may feel like too much trouble. Use the canteens, if any, if the food is bearable, especially at the beginning. As well as being fed, it will give you the opportunity to meet people and make friends.

Meet people

Seek out other newcomers. Loneliness can make the challenges of your new life seem much worse. Yet when you start, everyone is alone. Colleges recognise this and often organise 'getting to know you' social events, 'freshers' fairs'. Take advantage of these and any other social opportunities. The very beginning of your first term, when you first arrive, is a key time for making friends. Use strategies like propping your door open, if you are in a hall of residence, to encourage people to drop in and get to know you.

If you are shy and find it very difficult to join in, remember other students will be feeling nervous too, and trying to hide it. If there is something that especially interests you, such as music or a sport, find out if there's a college society that focuses on this. Meeting people with similar interests and outlooks makes life seem more manageable.

If you have moved to a new town, live with others to start with, if at all possible. If you can't get a place in a hall of residence or student flat, try and find a flatshare. Avoid being isolated in a bedsit, where there are no other students. That way you avoid loneliness, and share housework and meals.

Finances

In the last ten or 15 years, since student loans were introduced, there has been an increase in students taking on paid employment alongside their studying. Also, many mature students are already in full-time employment and may only be studying part time. Studying is now more expensive than ever and there is often concern about the debt that will be waiting at the end of a course of study.

Make sure you find out about all of the financial help you are entitled to. Nearly all universities now have a special finance service that can help you find out if you are receiving the right type and amount of loans or funding for your personal situation. If you are a mature student, already in work, find out if your employer will sponsor your studies – they may have a funded 'personal development scheme' or they may be willing to pay for studies that give you skills that will help you to work better for them.

However you are funding your studies, don't wait until any money problems get out of control. Seek advice as early as possible, so that you can continue your studies without worrying whether you can pay your rent or buy food.

➪ The above information is reprinted from the Mind booklet *How to cope with the stress of student life* © Mind 2010. Visit www.mind.org.uk for more information on a wide range of mental health topics.

© Mind

MIND

KEY FACTS

⇨ A recent survey estimated that during 2008 and 2009, over 400,000 people in Britain experienced work-related stress that was making them unwell. Another survey from 2009 found that around one in six workers thought that their job was stressful. (page 1)

⇨ Financial worry was the issue most likely to cause sleepless nights for Brits, according to research by YouGov. (page 2)

⇨ If you experience stress over a long period, or you have severe stress, you may develop other conditions as a result. (page 4)

⇨ Estimates indicate that self-reported work-related stress, depression or anxiety accounted for an estimated 13.5 million lost working days in Britain in 2007/08. (page 5)

⇨ Three out of four men in Britain say they would not go to the GP if they were under stress as they would be afraid that the GP would think that they are 'unbalanced' or 'neurotic'. (page 6)

⇨ About one in every ten people will have troublesome anxiety or a phobia at some point in their lives. However, most of us never ask for treatment. (page 10)

⇨ Some of us seem to be born with a tendency to be anxious – research suggests that it can be inherited through our genes. However, even people who are not naturally anxious can become anxious if they are put under enough pressure. (page 11)

⇨ Generalised anxiety disorder (GAD) develops in about one in 50 people at some stage in life. Twice as many women as men are affected. It usually first develops in your 20s and is less common in older people. (page 14)

⇨ People with GAD are more likely than average to smoke heavily, drink too much alcohol and take street drugs. Each of these things may ease anxiety symptoms in the short-term. (page 15)

⇨ The physical symptoms that occur with panic attacks do not mean there is a physical problem with the heart, chest, etc. The symptoms mainly occur because of an 'overdrive' of nervous impulses from the brain to various parts of the body during a panic attack. (page 16)

⇨ It is estimated that about 13.4 million working days are lost each year through anxiety and stress-related conditions, and stress-related illness costs employers in Great Britain more than £3.7 billion a year. (page 17)

⇨ For each of us, there is 'good stress' as well as 'bad stress' – for example, being under pressure to get something done may motivate you to get it done. However, some experiences – such as being made redundant or being bereaved – can have a negative effect. (page 18)

⇨ Money worries are the main concern of stressed-out Britons, according to the results of a poll which reveals that as many as 40 million adults admit to suffering from some form of regular anxiety. (page 21)

⇨ Fathers work longer hours than childless men. One in three fathers work more than a 48-hour week, while one in four men without children work more than 48 hours per week. 12 per cent of fathers work more than 60 hours per week. (page 22)

⇨ There is now convincing evidence that prolonged periods of stress, including work-related stress, have an adverse effect on physical and mental health and well-being. (page 24)

⇨ A growing body of scientific evidence suggests that not only can stress bring about permanent changes in your body, but you can even pass on some of those changes to your offspring. (page 30)

⇨ Under-25s are the most stressed age group overall and the most stressed about unemployment. (page 35)

⇨ A study has shown that people who were regularly active in their spare time had less likelihood of being depressed and anxious. (page 37)

Angst

A feeling of anxiety or apprehension.

Anxiety

Anxiety can be described as a feeling of fear, apprehension, tension and/or stress. Most people experience anxiety from time to time and this is a perfectly normal response to stress. However, some individuals suffer from anxiety disorders which cause them to experience symptoms such as intense, persistent fear or nervousness, panic attacks and hyperventilation.

Cardiovascular disease

Conditions that affect the heart and circulation.

Cognitive behavioural therapy (CBT)

Cognitive behavioural therapy (CBT) describes a number of therapies that are designed to solve problems. CBT starts with the idea that your problems are often created by you. It is not the situation itself that is making you unhappy, but how you think about it and react to it. CBT aims to change the way that you think about a situation, as well as influencing your behaviour.

Depression

Someone is said to be significantly depressed, or suffering from depression, when feelings of sadness or misery don't go away quickly and are so bad that they interfere with everyday life. Symptoms can also include low self-esteem and a lack of motivation.

'Fight or flight' response

Also called the stress response, this refers to a physical reaction the body encounters when faced with something it perceives to be a threat. The nervous system is primed, preparing the body to either fight the threat or run away from it. In the past, this response would have helped human beings to survive threats such as predatory animals. While this no longer applies to our modern lifestyles, our bodies will still react with the fight-or-flight response to any perceived threat – an approaching deadline, for example – causing many of the negative symptoms of stress.

Generalised anxiety disorder (GAD)

Someone with GAD has a lot of anxiety (feeling fearful, worried and tense) on most days, and not just in specific situations, and the condition persists long-term. Some of the physical symptoms of anxiety come and go. Someone with this high level of 'background anxiety' may also have panic attacks and some phobias.

Panic attack

A panic attack is a severe attack of anxiety and fear which occurs suddenly, often without warning, and for no apparent reason. Symptoms can include palpitations, sweating, trembling, nausea and hyperventilation. At least one in ten people have occasional panic attacks. They tend to occur most in young adults.

Phobia

A fear of a situation or thing that is not actually dangerous and which most people do not find troublesome. The nearer a phobic person gets to the situation or thing that makes them anxious, the more anxious they get, and so they tend to avoid it. Away from the thing or situation that makes them feel anxious, they feel fine.

Stress

Stress is the feeling of being under pressure. A little bit of pressure can be a good thing, helping to motivate you: however, too much pressure or prolonged pressure can lead to stress, which is unhealthy for the mind and body and can cause symptoms such as lack of sleep, loss of appetite and difficulty concentrating.

ACKNOWLEDGEMENTS

The publisher is grateful for permission to reproduce the following material.

While every care has been taken to trace and acknowledge copyright, the publisher tenders its apology for any accidental infringement or where copyright has proved untraceable. The publisher would be pleased to come to a suitable arrangement in any such case with the rightful owner.

Chapter One: Stress and Anxiety

Stress, © Crown copyright is reproduced with the permission of Her Majesty's Stationery Office – nhs.uk, *Facts about stress,* © International Stress Management Association UK, *The stigma of stress,* © Crown copyright is reproduced with the permission of Her Majesty's Stationery Office – nhs.uk, *Work-related stress – signs and symptoms,* © Crown copyright is reproduced with the permission of Her Majesty's Stationery Office, *Anxiety, panic and phobias,* © Royal College of Psychiatrists, *Generalised anxiety disorder (GAD),* © EMIS 2010, as distributed at http://www.patient.co.uk/health/Anxiety-Generalised-Anxiety-Disorder, used with permission, *Panic attacks,* © EMIS 2011, as distributed at http://www.patient.co.uk/health/Panic-Attack.htm, used with permission.

Chapter Two: Causes of Stress

What makes you stressed?, © British Heart Foundation, *Money worries top Britons' stress lists,* © Guardian News and Media Limited 2010, *Stress, guilt and exhaustion 'toxic mix' for middle-class parents,* © Demos, *Workplace stress,* © NHS Health Scotland, *Summary of the law on stress at work,* © Thompsons Solicitors LLP, *Common causes of stress at work,* © Crown copyright is reproduced with the permission of Her Majesty's Stationery Office, *Stressed out? It could be in your genes,* © The Independent.

Chapter Three: Learning to Cope

What can you do about stress?, © British Heart Foundation, *British approach to dealing with stress runs risk of serious mental health problems,* © Mental Health Foundation, *Anxiety eased by exercise,* © hc2d.co.uk, *How to cope with the stress of student life,* © Mind.

Illustrations

Pages 1, 15, 23, 39: Don Hatcher; pages 3, 20, 26, 33: Simon Kneebone; pages 7, 21, 31, 36: Angelo Madrid; pages 17, 24: Bev Aisbett.

Cover photography

Left: © David Ritter. Centre: © George Crux. Right: © Catalina González Carrasco (www.ficto.net).

Additional acknowledgements

Research by Shivonne Gates.

With thanks to the Independence team: Mary Chapman, Sandra Dennis and Jan Sunderland.

Lisa Firth
Cambridge
April, 2011

ASSIGNMENTS

The following tasks aim to help you think through the issues surrounding stress and anxiety and provide a better understanding of the topic.

1 Create a booklet to help students who are at risk of exam stress. Provide broad information on how to cope with stress, including relaxation techniques, tips on nutrition, advice on how best to prepare for an exam and anything else you think your readers would find helpful – you could even include some stress-busting meal ideas or suggest a relaxation playlist! Keep the tone light and fun and include illustrations.

2 Make a list of the most common causes of stress. Select one item from your list and brainstorm the issue. How many people in the UK suffer from stress as a result of this problem? How could it be avoided? What are the most effective solutions to stress arising from this issue?

3 Do you think modern life is more stressful than life in the UK 50 years ago? Speak to people you know who were young adults during the 1950s and 60s. Do they feel life was more or less stressful at that time than it has been for subsequent generations?

4 Consider our attitude to stress in the western world. Is stress also an issue in developing countries?

5 'We all get stressed from time to time, but most people manage to deal with it without counselling or treatment. People suffering from stress should stop being self-indulgent and pull themselves together.' Do you think this view is too harsh or do you think it has a point? Can you understand why some people are still embarrassed to discuss the highly stigmatised issue of stress? Discuss your views with a partner.

6 Find out more about cognitive behavioural therapy (CBT). What does this treatment involve and how can it help people to deal with stress and anxiety symptoms?

7 'Stress is an illness of the mind. It is not physically dangerous.' Using *Work-related stress – signs and symptoms* on pages 7-9 as a starting point, write a rebuttal of this statement outlining how stress can be physically as well as mentally damaging.

8 Read *Anxiety, panic and phobias* on pages 10-13. Write definitions of the following terms in your own words, clearly stating the distinctions between them: stress; anxiety; panic; phobia; generalised anxiety disorder.

9 Read through the 'Am I stressed?' quiz on pages 19-20. Devise your own quiz specifically for the 16-18 age group which could help to diagnose stress. Think about the most likely causes of stress among this age group – for example, exams, coursework, relationships – and incorporate these into the questions.

10 Read *Money worries top Britons' stress lists* on page 21. Carry out a similar poll among friends, peers and family members to ascertain what they feel is their biggest source of stress (try to include respondents from a number of age groups in your survey). Do your results tally with those described in the article? Create a selection of graphs displaying your findings, showing the results by age group and gender.

11 List what you think would be the five most stressful jobs to have. Why did you choose these professions?

12 Write a guide for managers, outlining how to spot stress in the workplace; the most effective way to deal with this; their legal obligations regarding workplace stress, and the benefits arising to their business if they tackle stress successfully (for example, fewer staff absences).

13 What is post-traumatic stress disorder (PTSD), what generally causes it and how is it treated?

14 Design a 'Cook Yourself Calm Cookbook', containing recipes to help beat stress. Bear in mind that if the readers have a lot of stress in their lives, they are unlikely to have much time for food preparation: they will want recipes which are nutritious, filling and quick to prepare. Read the 'Eat well' section of *What can you do about stress?* on page 33 as a starting point.

15 Do you ever feel stressed? Keep a stress diary for a fortnight, recording every time you felt stressed, what caused it and how you reacted. Review your diary: is there anything you could change in your life to avoid stress?